VOICES

FROM OUR NATION

Program Consultants

Joseph D. Baca, New Mexico State Department of Education

Catharine D. Bell, University of Chicago Laboratory Schools

David L. Depew, Ector County ISD, Odessa, Texas

Miriam M. Glessner, Public Schools, Columbus, Ohio

Gloria P. Hagans, Public Schools, Norfolk, Virginia

Anthony La Rocca, Bellmore, New York

Norman McRae, Detroit Public Schools

Audrey Tieger, President, California Council for the Social Studies

Theron Trimble, Collier County Public Schools, Naples, Florida

Acknowledgments

Project Editor: Anne Souby

Product Development: Learning Design Associates, Inc.

Cover Design: Joyce Spicer

Cover Artist: Susan Melrath

Title page photo: The Granger Collection, New York.

Library of Congress Cataloging-in-Publication Data
Voices from our nation / written by Steck-Vaughn Company.
p.   cm. — (Voices)
Includes index.
Summary: Presents a view of American history through the words, songs, letters, diaries, and other documents of individuals such as pilgrims, pioneers, explorers, slaves, Native Americans, politicians, and astronauts.
  ISBN 0-8114-2771-4
1. United States — History — Sources — Juvenile literature. 2. American letters — Juvenile literature. 3. American diaries — Juvenile literature. 4. Speeches, addresses, etc., American — Juvenile literature. 5. Songs, English — United States — Texts. [1. United States — History — Sources.] I. Steck-Vaughn Company. II. Series: Voices (Austin, Tex.)
E173.V63   1990

973—dc20   90 – 41623 CIP AC

1 2 3 4 5 6 7 8 9 0   95 94 93 92 91 90

CONTENTS

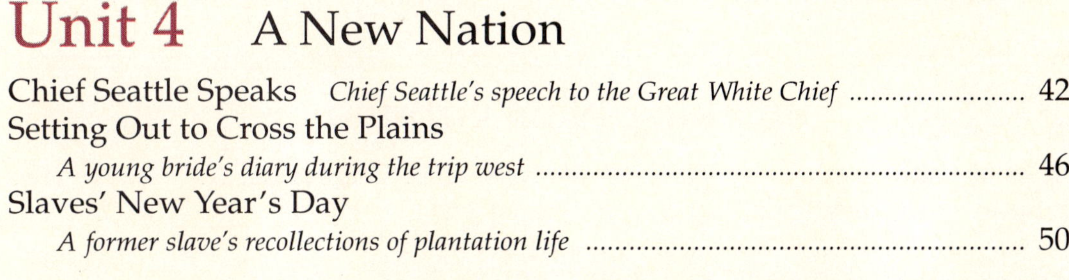

INTRODUCTION

History is the story of many different people. American history is the story of Vikings and Pilgrims, soldiers and slaves, Native Americans and immigrants from a hundred countries. These are the people who built our nation. Their experiences are the very fabric of the American story.

The best way to learn about history is to listen to the people who lived it. In *Voices* people from the past speak in their own words—about their lives and the time they lived in. Through their letters, diaries, speeches, and songs, you'll hear their voices. You'll learn about their thoughts, lives, feelings, and dreams. *Voices* is a tapestry of living history.

In these pages you can come ashore in the New World with Christopher Columbus after two long months at sea. Share the Pilgrims' struggles at Plymouth. Sing the songs of the American Revolution. Witness the tragedy at Wounded Knee with Black Elk. Chuckle at a former slave's clever response to his past master's job offer. Travel west in a wagon with a young bride. Soar with a World War I ace pilot. Experience the bombing of Pearl Harbor through the eyes of a sixteen-year-old civilian. Feel the racial tension of the 1950s with a black student at Little Rock. Blast off into space with astronaut Sally Ride.

Each reading starts with a short introduction. This paragraph helps to set the scene. The paragraph at the end of each reading reveals what happened next. Timelines and maps pinpoint the sequence and location of events. Margin notes define unfamiliar words.

The voices in this book tell about the way things used to be. Each voice reveals a different view of American history. Together they prove how much alike people are, no matter when or where they lived. Sometimes inspiring, sometimes tragic, these are voices from the past that speak to us today.

EXPLORING AMERICA

Early explorers knew very little about the continents of North and South America. This map comes from a globe made in 1520. It shows the islands of the West Indies and South America.

Vikings: sailors from northernmost Europe who raided the coasts of Europe from the late 700s to the 900s

Scandinavia: region made up of present-day Norway, Sweden, and Denmark

Greenland: largest island in the world, located northeast of North America; mostly ice covered

Some 500 years before Columbus set out on his voyages, **Vikings** came ashore in northeastern North America. A bold seafaring people from **Scandinavia**, they set up a colony in **Greenland** first. Sailing farther west, they found a green and wooded land. But they left their settlements there after about 15 years.

By the time Columbus set sail in 1492, trade already linked Europe and Asia. Many Europeans enjoyed spices, silks, and fine cottons from the Far East. But the cost was high. The trade routes, over both sea and land, were long and full of danger. Furthermore, merchants from the Middle East and Italy controlled these routes. They charged high prices and made large profits.

Some European rulers hired explorers to search for new trade routes. A daring Italian explorer named Christopher Columbus was among these. He tried to reach Asia by sailing directly west from Europe. In 1492 he and his crew came upon islands in the Atlantic Ocean. They were just off the coast of two huge continents

1000	1100	1200	1300

1002? **Leif Ericson winters in North America.**

unknown to most Europeans. These continents, North and South America, came to be known as the New World.

After Columbus's discovery European rulers were eager to send ships across the Atlantic. At first Spain and Portugal led the race to the New World. By the early 1600s Great Britain, France, and the Netherlands had all claimed parts of the Americas.

Explorers of this time had a thirst for knowledge. But they had also heard rumors of gold and silver to be found in the Americas. They wanted to find land and wealth. Determined to defeat anyone who stood in their way, they brought armies of soldiers. Two large empires of Native Americans—the Inca and the Aztec— were all but destroyed.

The first European explorers in the New World probably arrived on Viking ships. They left their homes in search of new lands and adventure.

This unit describes the explorations of Europeans in the new land across the sea.

- An old Scandinavian story describes the first European explorations of the New World by **Leif Ericson.**
- In his journal **Christopher Columbus** writes about discovering land after two months at sea.
- An eyewitness gives an account of the first European expedition into the North American mainland by **Hernando De Soto**.

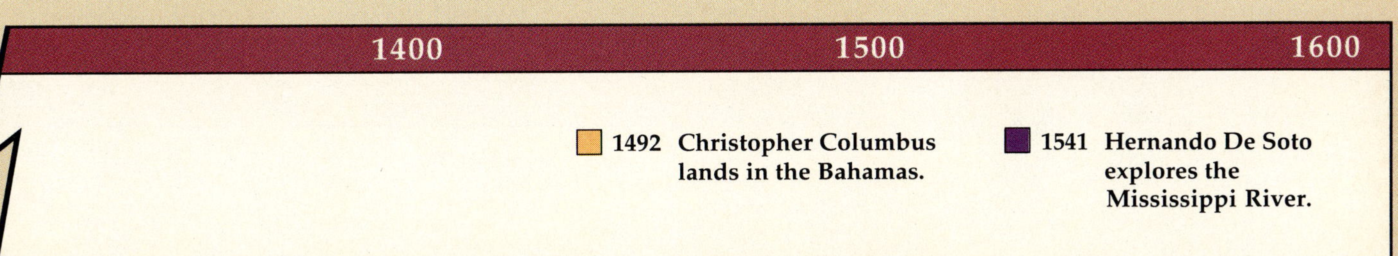

The Naming of Vinland

Leif Ericson

Viking explorer Leif Ericson was probably the first European to explore the coast of North America.

Five hundred years before Columbus set foot in the New World, the Vikings explored the North American coast. Around 1002 Leif Ericson sailed west from a Viking colony in Greenland. His explorations are described in the Icelandic **sagas**. These stories blend history and fantasy. They were written a hundred years or more after Ericson died.

There was now great talk of discovering new countries, and nowhere did men talk more of this than at **Brattahlid**.

Above all others, Leif, the son of **Eirik** the Red, desired to make a voyage westward and explore the new lands. He was a man of striking appearance, tall and powerful with piercing blue eyes and a fine head of **flaxen** hair. He was a generous and faithful friend, but a **ruthless** enemy who could strike or throw with either hand. He was outstandingly skillful in the **seaman's art** and the first captain to make direct voyages between Greenland, Scotland, Norway, and back again.

Leif went to see Bjarni Herjolfsson and talked long with him. He bought Bjarni's ship with the dragon **prow** and engaged a crew of thirty-five men. They were men of ability and experience. . . .

They made the ship ready and put out to sea. The wind and the waves were with them and they came first to that land which Bjarni had sighted last. Leif was at the **tiller** and he brought the ship close up to the shore. They cast anchor, lowered a boat, and rowed ashore. Great glaciers rose

sagas: stories about Vikings

Brattahlid: Viking settlement in Greenland

Eirik: (Eric)

flaxen: pale yellow

ruthless: cruel

seaman's art: handling of a ship

prow: the forward part of a ship

tiller: handle for steering a ship

985

985? Eric the Red colonizes Greenland.

990? Bjarni Herjolfsson sights the mainland of North America.

before them. Between the glaciers and the sea the land was like one great slab of rock. Not a blade of grass was to be seen. A worthless country they all agreed, **barren** and useless.

"At least," said Leif, "we have done better than Bjarni by this country—we have set foot on it. I shall give this place a name and call it Helluland, Stoneland."

They rowed back to their ship and put out to sea. On the morning of the third day they sighted a second land. Once again Leif sailed right up to it, cast anchor, and led a party of men ashore. Wherever they went they found white sandy beaches sloping gently to the sea. The country itself was flat and heavily wooded.

"This country," said Leif, "shall be named in accordance with its nature: it shall be called Markland, Forestland."

A northeast wind was rising and they hurried back to the ship as fast as they could.

For two days they sailed with this northeast wind before sighting land. Leif, who was famous for his eyesight, saw land first. They sailed toward it and cast anchor off an island to the north of the mainland. They went ashore in fine weather and looked about them. The dew lay heavy on the grass and the men got their hands wet with it. Those who tasted the dew said they had never known anything as sweet. Then they returned to their ship and sailed into the **sound** that lay between the island and a **cape** jutting north from the mainland.

Leif steered a westerly course around the cape. There were extensive shallows there, and at low tide they found themselves left **high and dry** with the sea

barren: not able to produce crops or fruit

sound: long narrow strip of water

cape: a point of land extending into the water. Historians believe Leif may have sailed as far south as Cape Cod.

high and dry: unable to sail because the water was so shallow

The Vikings were sailors and navigators. They built strong ocean-going ships and sailed west to explore Iceland, Greenland, and the coast of North America.

1300

1002? **Leif Ericson and his men sail west of Greenland and winter in Vinland.**

1200s **The Icelandic sagas describe the travels of the Vikings.**

almost out of sight. Everyone was so eager to go ashore that they could not summon up the patience to wait for the rising tide to float the ship. Instead they raced to the land at a place where a river flowed out of a lake. As soon as the tide rose under the ship, they took their boat and rowed out to it. Then they brought the ship up the river and anchored it in the lake and carried their sleeping bags ashore. First they built small houses of wood and **turf** and then they set out to inspect the country about them more closely.

There was no lack of salmon in the river and lake—bigger salmon than any of them had ever seen. Leif observed this plentiful source of food, noted the forest thick with trees and no doubt filled with game. He called the crew to him and suggested that they winter here. All thirty-five of his shipmates agreed and they set to work building a main house.

When they were finished with the big house Leif once again called them together and made a second announcement. "I want to divide our company into two groups and have this land explored. Half of you will remain here while the other half will go exploring. Never go so far that home cannot be reached by evening and never become separated one from another. I myself will take turns exploring and staying here."

They found a kind land where there was no frost and the grass hardly withered. Livestock would need no winter **fodder** here. There were rolling grasslands and meadows rich with wild wheat. Day and night were of more equal length than in Greenland or Iceland. On the shortest day of winter the sun was up when they ate their morning meal and was still visible by the middle of the afternoon.

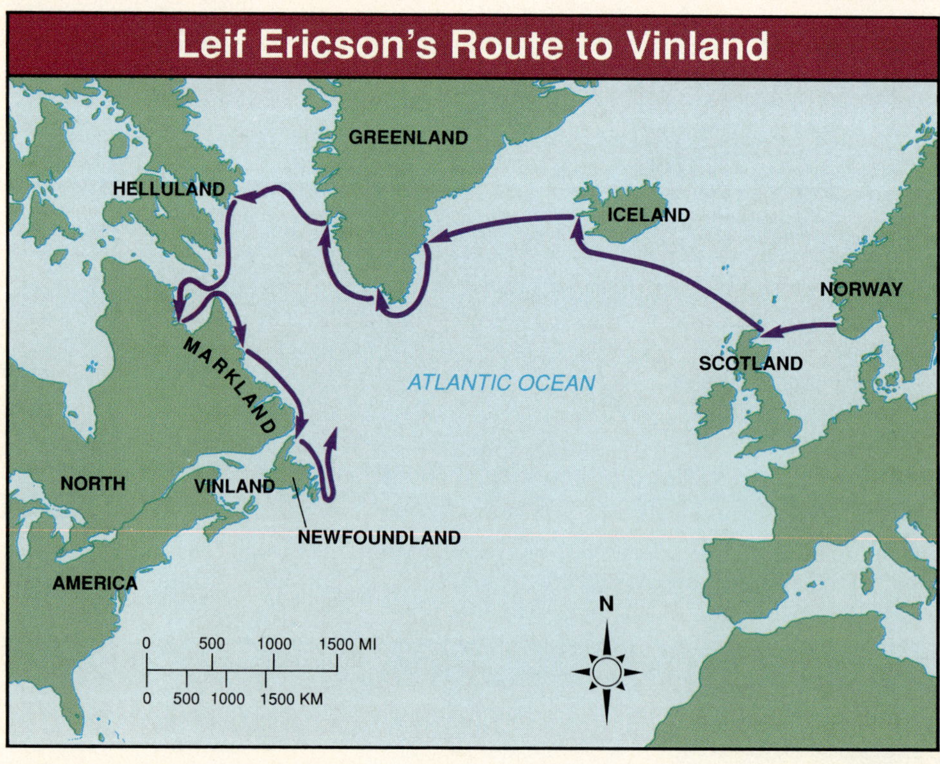

One evening toward the end of winter the group that had been exploring returned without one man. Leif was angry when he saw that the missing man was Tyrkir the German.

"All of you know that Tyrkir is Eirik the Red's most trusted servant and my **foster father.** None of you are ignorant of my feelings toward him, and yet you let him wander **astray.** He has been with my family since I was a child in Iceland and I shall not return home without him."

So saying, Leif turned away and made ready to go out searching for Tyrkir. Twelve men went with him. But when they had gone only a short distance from the big house, there was Tyrkir coming to meet them. His welcome was a warm one. Leif quickly realized that his foster father was in high spirits.

Tyrkir had a big forehead, little eyes, and not much more of a face besides. Although short and insignificant-looking, he was a master craftsman. During the winter months he had made, among other things, carved **gable heads** from the native maple wood.

Leif said to him, "Why are you so late, foster father? And how did you get separated from your companions?"

Tyrkir answered readily and at great length, rolling his eyes and making funny faces all the

The Viking alphabet was made up of letters called runes. Runes were found on this gravestone in Sweden.

while. His listeners were amused but did not learn much, since he was speaking in German. At last Tyrkir spoke in Icelandic.

"I did not go much beyond where we are now, yet I saw something no one else has seen." Tyrkir grinned. "I have found vines and grapes."

"Is that true, foster father?" asked Leif.

"Of course it is true. You forget that where I was born grapes and wine are no **rarity.**"

The next morning Leif said to his comrades, "I have found a name for this land that is worthy of the good things we have found here. It shall be called Vinland."

The men agreed that Vinland was a fitting name for the country.

Leif Ericson made no maps of his voyages. Therefore, scholars are not certain where in North America he landed. Archaeologists discovered the ruins of a **Norse** settlement in northern Newfoundland in the 1960s. Some scholars think that this was the area the Vikings called Vinland. Others think that Vinland was farther south near Cape Cod.

The Discovery of the Bahamas

Christopher Columbus was a skilled sailor with a thirst for adventure. This portrait was painted 30 years after he died.

> " It is a pleasure to gaze upon this place because it is all so green. . . . "

Christopher Columbus

Sponsored by King Ferdinand and Queen Isabella of Spain, Christopher Columbus first crossed the Atlantic Ocean in 1492. He was searching for a short route to the Indies—India, China, and Japan. On this trip Columbus wrote down each day what happened and what he saw. He was one of the first sailors to keep a log, or journal.

WSW: the direction west southwest

barnacles: shellfish that grow on rocks and ship bottoms

vespers: evening prayers

ever-vigilant: watchful

Thursday, 11 October 1492

I sailed to the **WSW**, and we took more water aboard than at any other time on the voyage. I saw several things that were indications of land. At one time a large flock of sea birds flew overhead, and a green reed was found floating near the ship. The crew of the *Pinta* spotted some of the same reeds and some other plants; they also saw what looked like a small board or plank. A stick was recovered that looks manmade, perhaps carved with an iron tool. Those on the *Niña* saw a little stick covered with **barnacles**. I am certain that many things were overlooked because of the heavy sea, but even these few made the crew breathe easier; in fact, the men have even become cheerful. I sailed 81 miles from sunset yesterday to sunset today. As is our custom, **vespers** were said in the late afternoon, and a special thanksgiving was offered to God for giving us renewed hope through the many signs of land He has provided.

After sunset I ordered the pilot to return to my original westerly course, and I urged the crew to be **ever-vigilant.** I took the added precaution of doubling

Aug. 1492

Aug. The *Niña,* the *Pinta,* and the *Santa María* sail from Spain.	**Sept.** The ships complete three weeks of the voyage with no land in sight.	**Oct.** The fleet sights land at 2 A.M. on October 12. Before noon Columbus goes ashore.

"

the number of lookouts, and I reminded the men that the first to sight land would be given a silk **doublet** as a personal token from me. Further, he would be given an **annuity** of 10,000 **maravedíes** from the **Sovereigns**.

About 10 o'clock at night, while standing on the **sterncastle**, I thought I saw a light to the west. It looked like a little wax candle bobbing up and down. It had the same appearance as a light or torch belonging to fishermen or travellers who alternately raised and lowered it, or perhaps were going from house to house. I am the first to admit that I was so eager to find land that I did not trust my own senses, so I called for Pedro Gutiérrez, the representative of the King's household, and asked him to watch for the light. After a few moments, he too saw it. I then summoned Rodrigo Sánchez of **Segovia**, the **comptroller** of the fleet, and asked him to watch for the light. He saw nothing, nor did any other member of the crew. It was such an uncertain thing that I did not feel it was adequate proof of land.

The moon, in its third quarter, rose in the east shortly before midnight. I estimate that we were making about 9 **knots** and had gone some $67\frac{1}{2}$ miles between the beginning of night and 2 o'clock in the morning. Then, at two hours after midnight, the *Pinta* fired a cannon, my prearranged signal for the sighting of land.

I now believe that the light I saw earlier was a sign from God and that it was truly the first positive indication of land. When we caught up with the *Pinta*, which was always running ahead because she was a swift sailer, I learned that the first man to sight

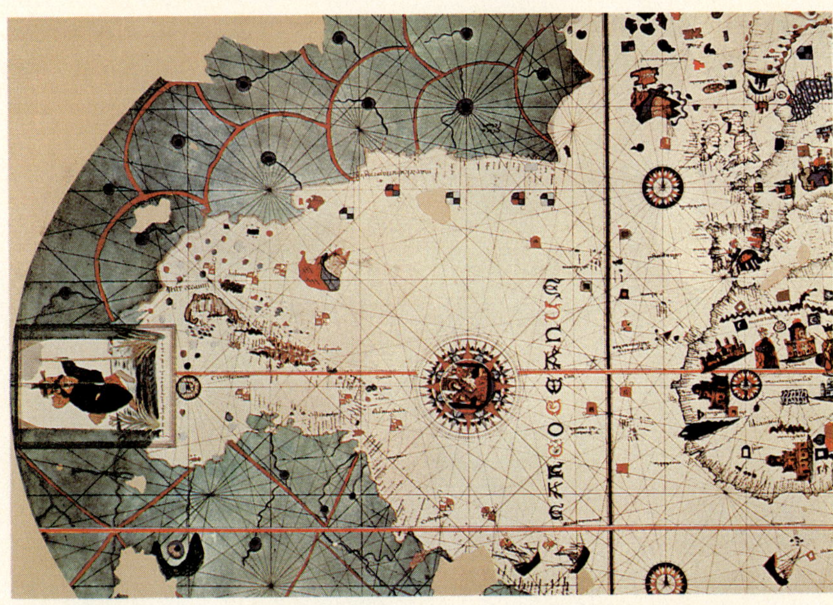

One of Columbus's navigators drew this map. It shows part of Europe on the right. On the left are the islands that Columbus discovered in the New World.

Mar. 1493

Nov. Columbus begins to explore islands near Cuba. He sets up crosses wherever he goes.

Dec. The *Santa María* wrecks on a reef near present-day Haiti. Natives help save its cargo.

Jan. The ships begin their voyage home.
Mar. Columbus arrives back in Spain.

land was Rodrigo de Triana, a seaman from **Lepe**.

I hauled in all sails but the mainsail and **lay-to** till daylight. The land is about 6 miles to the west.

Friday, 12 October 1492

At dawn we saw naked people, and I went ashore in the ship's boat, armed, followed by Martín Alonso Pinzón, captain of the *Pinta*, and his brother, Vincente Yáñez Pinzón, captain of the *Niña*. I **unfurled** the royal banner and the captains brought the flags which displayed a large green cross with the letters **F and Y** at the left and right side of the cross. Over each letter was the appropriate crown of that Sovereign. These flags were carried as a standard on all of the ships. After a prayer of thanksgiving I ordered the captains of the *Pinta* and *Niña*, together with Rodrigo de Escobedo (secretary of the fleet), and Rodrigo Sánchez of Segovia (comptroller of the fleet) to bear faith and witness that I was taking possession of this island for the King and Queen. I made all the necessary **declarations** and had these **testimonies** carefully written down by the secretary. In addition to those named above, the entire company of the fleet **bore witness to** this act. To this island I gave the name *San Salvador,* in honor of our Blessed Lord.

No sooner had we concluded the formalities of taking possession of the island than people began to come to the beach, all as naked as their mothers bore them, and the women also, although I did not see more than one very young girl. All those that I saw were young people, none of whom was over 30 years old. They are very well-built people, with handsome bodies and very fine faces, though their appearance is **marred** somewhat by very broad heads and foreheads, more so than I have ever seen in any other race. Their eyes are large and very

When Columbus stepped ashore at San Salvador, he thought he had landed on an island off the coast of Asia. He carried a royal banner to claim the land for Spain.

pretty, and their skin is the color of **Canary Islanders** or of sunburned peasants, not at all black, as would be expected because we are on an east-west line with **Hierro** in the Canaries. These are tall people and their legs, with no exceptions, are quite straight, and none of them has a **paunch**. They are, in fact, **well proportioned**. Their hair is not kinky, but straight, and coarse like horsehair. They wear it short over the eyebrows, but they have a long **hank** in the back that they never cut. Many of the natives paint their faces; others paint their whole bodies; some, only the eyes or nose. Some are painted black, some white, some red; others are of different colors.

Columbus called the people he met in the New World *Indians* because he thought he had landed in the East Indies.

The people here called this island *Guanahaní* in their language, and their speech is very fluent, although I do not understand any of it. They are friendly and **well-dispositioned** people who **bare no arms** except for small spears, and they have no iron. I showed one my sword, and through ignorance he grabbed it by the blade and cut himself. Their spears are made of wood, to which they attach a fish tooth at one end, or some other sharp thing.

I want the natives to develop a friendly attitude toward us because I know that they are a people who can be made free and converted to our Holy Faith more by love than by force. I therefore gave red caps to some and glass beads to others. They hung the beads around their necks, along with some other things of slight value that I gave them. And they took great pleasure in this and became so friendly that it was a marvel. They traded and gave everything they had with good will, but it seems to me that they have very little and are poor in everything. I warned my men to take nothing from the people without giving something in exchange.

This afternoon the people of San Salvador came swimming to our ships and in boats made from one log. They brought us parrots, balls of cotton thread, spears, and many other things, including a kind of **dry leaf** that they **hold in great esteem**. For these items we swapped them little glass beads and **hawks' bells**.

Many of the men I have seen have scars on their bodies, and when I made signs to them to find out how this happened, they indicated that people from other nearby islands come to San Salvador to capture them; they defend themselves the best they can. I believe that people from the mainland come here to take them as slaves. They ought to make good and skilled servants, for they repeat very quickly whatever we

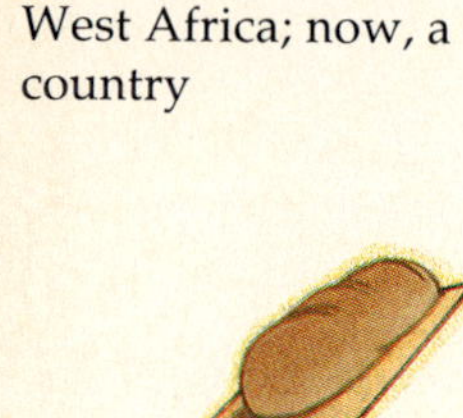

say to them. I think they can easily be made Christians, for they seem to have no religion. If it pleases Our Lord, I will take six of them to Your Highnesses when I depart, in order that they may learn our language.

Saturday, 13 October 1492
After sunrise people from San Salvador again began to come to our ships in boats **fashioned** in one piece from the trunks of trees. These boats are wonderfully made, considering the country we are in, and every bit as fine as those I have seen in **Guinea**. They come in all sizes. Some can carry 40 or 50 men; some are so small that only one man rides in it. The men move very swiftly over the water, rowing with a blade that looks like a **baker's peel**. They do not use **oarlocks**, but dip the peel in the water and push themselves forward. If a boat **capsizes** they all

begin to swim, and they rock the boat until about half of the water is splashed out. Then they bail out the rest of the water with **gourds** that they carry for that purpose.

The people brought more balls of spun cotton, spears, and parrots. Other than the parrots, I have seen no beast of any kind on this island.

I have been very attentive and have tried very hard to find out if there is any gold here. I have seen a few natives who wear a little piece of gold hanging from a hole made in the nose. By signs, if I interpret them correctly, I have learned that by going to the south, or rounding the island to the south, I can find a king who possesses a lot of gold and has great containers of it. I have tried to find some natives who will take me to this great king, but none seems **inclined** to make the journey.

Tomorrow afternoon I intend

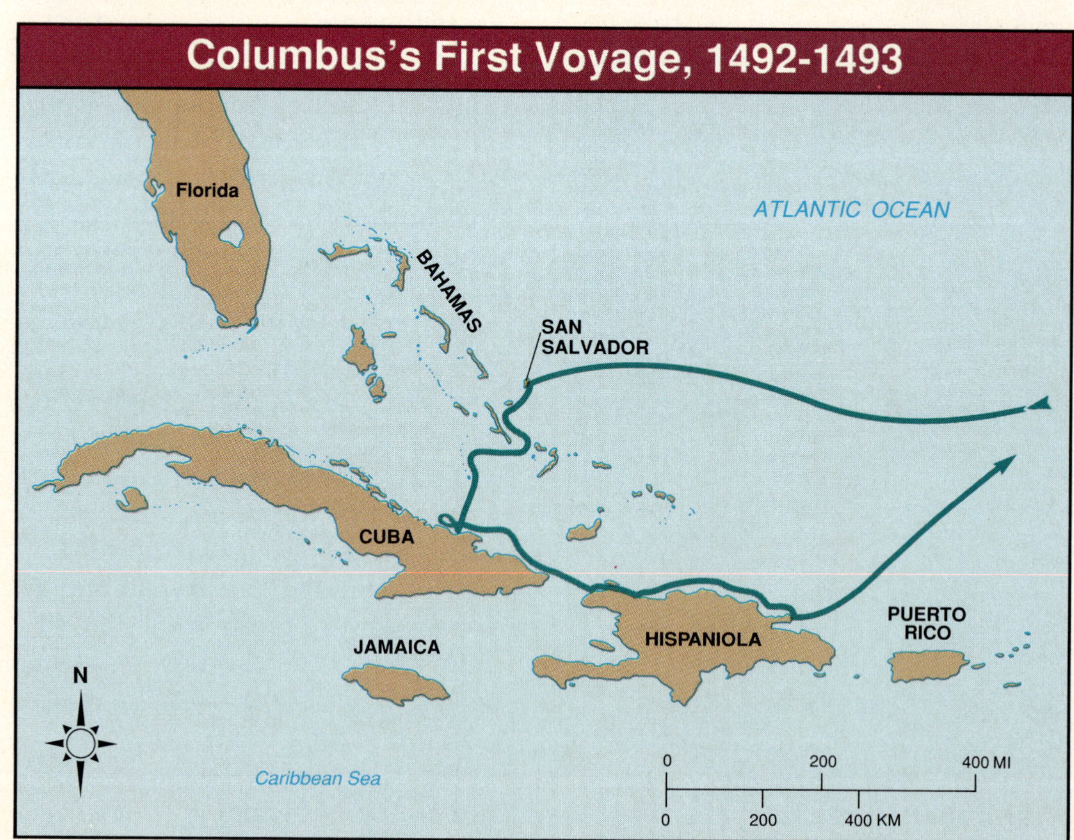

to go to the SW. The natives have indicated to me that not only is there land to the south and SW, but also to the NW. I shall go to the SW and look for gold and precious stones. Furthermore, if I understand correctly, it is from the NW that strangers come to fight and capture the people here.

This island is fairly large and very flat. It is green, with many trees and several bodies of water. There is a very large **lagoon** in the middle of the island and there are no mountains. It is a pleasure to gaze upon this place because it is all so green, and the weather is delightful. In fact, since we left the Canaries, God has not failed to provide one perfect day after the other.

I cannot get over the fact of how **docile** these people are. They have so little to give but will give it all for whatever we give them, if only broken pieces of glass and **crockery**. One seaman gave three Portuguese *ceitis* (not even worth a penny!) for about 25 pounds of spun cotton. I probably should have forbidden this exchange, but I wanted to take the cotton to Your Highnesses, and it seems to be in abundance. I think the cotton is grown on San Salvador, but I cannot say for sure because I have not been here that long. Also, the gold they wear hanging from their noses comes from here, but in order not to lose time I want to go to see if I can find the island of Japan.

lagoon: shallow lake or pond

docile: easy to manage or teach

crockery: pots, jars, or dishes made of baked clay

Columbus's command ship, the *Santa María,* sank near the island of Haiti in 1492.

Columbus made four voyages to the New World between 1492 and 1504. He never stopped believing that San Salvador was near Japan or China. By 1507 **Amerigo Vespucci** realized that Columbus had discovered a new continent. But the Native Americans came to be known as "Indians," and the islands Columbus first reached continue to be called the "West Indies."

Amerigo Vespucci: Italian navigator for whom America is named

Crossing the Great River

The Gentleman of Elvas

Hernando De Soto was the first European to see the mighty Mississippi River.

Hernando De Soto took part in the Spanish conquest of the Inca empire in South America during the 1530s. King Charles I of Spain asked De Soto to explore and conquer what is now the southern United States. De Soto led the first European expedition to reach the Mississippi River. An eyewitness describes how they crossed the river in 1541.

Quizquiz: may have been in present-day Arkansas

took: captured

cacique: chief

store: supply

league: old measure of distance, usually 2 to 3 miles

Great River: the Mississippi River

The Governor, De Soto, came to a town in the land of **Quizquiz** without being seen, and **took** all of the people in it before they came out of their houses. . . .

Six chief Indians came to the camp and said they had come to see what people we were. Long ago they had been told by their forefathers that a white people would conquer them. Therefore, they would return to their **cacique** and bid him come immediately to obey and serve De Soto. . . .

Because there was small **store** of corn where De Soto was staying, he moved to another town half a **league** from the **Great River**, where they found plenty. De Soto went to see the river, and found much timber near it to make barges, as well as good ground for a camp. Right away he moved there. They pitched their camp in a level field a crossbow shot from the river. They gathered all the corn of the towns they had passed lately, then began to cut timber and saw planks for barges. . . .

In the thirty days we were there, we made four barges. De Soto commanded four horsemen to enter each of three of them, three hours before daylight, with

1531

1531–36 De Soto serves as a leader in the conquest of the Incas.	**1537** King Charles I of Spain appoints De Soto governor of Cuba.

crossbowmen and rowers to set them on the other side. He sent men he trusted to land despite the Indians and seize the opposite shore or die in the attempt. . . . Because the stream was swift, they went a quarter of a league up the river along the bank, and crossing over, came down with the current, landing directly across from the camp. Before they reached land, the mounted horsemen left the barges for a sandy plot of very hard clear ground, where they all landed without any **resistance**. As soon as those who crossed first were on land . . . , the barges returned to where the Governor was, and within two hours after sunrise, all the men were over. . . .

The river was almost half a league wide. If a man stood still on the other side, it could not be told whether he was a man or no. The river was of great depth, and had a strong current. The water was always muddy. Many trees were brought downstream by the force of the water. There was a great store of fish in it, of several kinds, most of them differing from the freshwater fish of Spain.

resistance: fighting

For three years De Soto searched for gold in America. This painting by William H. Powell shows him riding into a village located on the Mississippi River.

De Soto continued exploring through what later became Arkansas and Louisiana. After his death in 1542 his soldiers feared Native Americans would attack once they heard De Soto was dead. So De Soto's men weighted his body and buried him in the Mississippi River. Luís de Moscoso took command of the expedition. He led the group back down the Mississippi River to the Gulf of Mexico.

From *Exploring the Great River*, pp. 8–13, adapted and edited by Robert Meredith and E. Brooks Smith. Copyright © 1969 by Robert K. Meredith and Edric B. Smith, Jr. By permission of Little, Brown and Company.

1542

1539 **De Soto lands in Florida.**

1541 **De Soto first sees the Mississippi River.**

1542 **De Soto dies and is buried in the Mississippi River.**

A NEW HOME IN A NEW WORLD

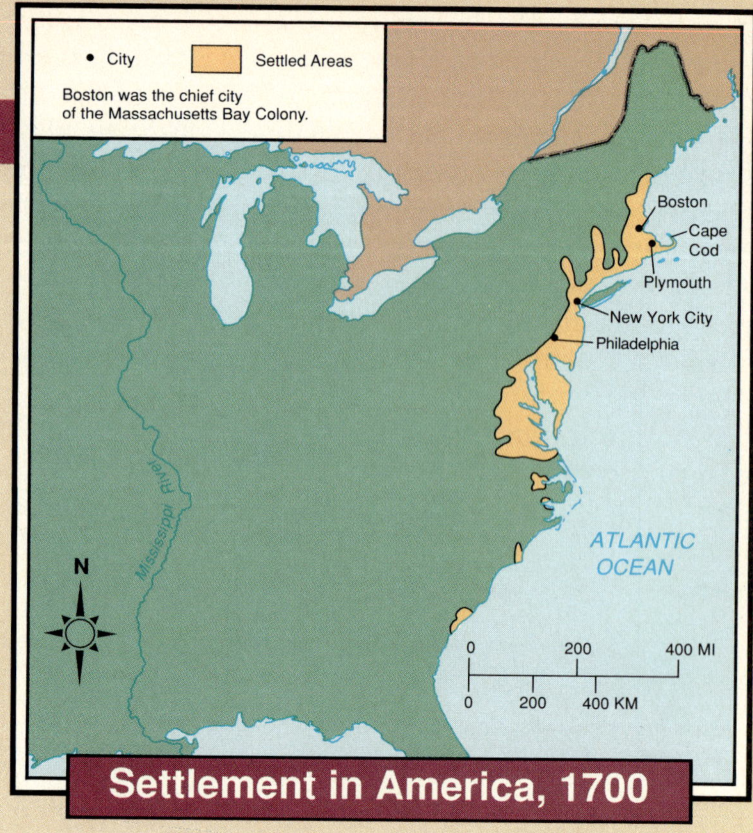

Settlement in America, 1700

The English began to colonize North America after they defeated the **Spanish Armada** in 1588. At this time the English began to believe they could compete with Spain and France for lands in the New World. They probably did not guess, though, that they would one day defeat both rivals and take over North America.

The English government wanted colonies so it could obtain new products to trade. It also wanted a place to sell British goods. But what did the colonists want? Many were seeking religious freedom. They wanted to live where they could worship in their own way. In England they could not do this. Other colonists hoped to find a better life. Many people in England were poor. If they could not pay the money they owed, they had to go to jail. In America these people had a chance to own their own land.

The men and women who settled North America were risk-takers. They were willing to face the unknown, to leave friends, family, and possessions behind. They were hard workers too. They

cleared land. They built towns. They set up laws and governed themselves.

The lives of the colonists, rich and poor, were shaped by the land. In the north farming was hard because of the poor, rocky soil. Colonists here soon turned to shipbuilding and fishing. Later manufacturing became important. Colonists in the south found the soil and climate ideal for growing tobacco, rice, and later cotton. These crops were grown on **plantations.** Slaves from Africa were the backbone of this economy. In the middle colonies many farmers grew corn and wheat. These "bread basket" colonies sold much of their crops to the other colonies.

The colonies grew rapidly. By 1700 the population was about 250,000. By then many people lived in busy cities. Philadelphia was the largest, followed by New York and Boston.

plantations: large estates on which crops are grown by workers who live on the estate

The village was the center of colonial life. Colonists often gathered on the village green after church on Sunday.

In this unit, three of these North American colonists describe life in the New World.

- **William Bradford** tells about the colonists' arrival at Plymouth, Massachusetts, and their plan to govern themselves.
- **John Winthrop,** a Massachusetts colonist, writes to his wife in England about what to bring when she joins him.
- **Benjamin Franklin,** inventor, statesman, publisher, and writer, offers witty advice to his fellow colonists.

1700	1750

1733 Benjamin Franklin publishes the first edition of *Poor Richard's Almanack.*

Pilgrims of Plymouth

William Bradford

While still on the *Mayflower*, Pilgrim leaders drew up and signed the Mayflower Compact, creating a government in the New World.

Separatists: people who wanted to separate from the Church of England to practice their own faith

In 1620 a group of **Separatists** set sail for the New World. They wanted to find a new home where they could worship freely. William Bradford helped found their colony, called Plymouth, and served as its governor for over 30 years. Bradford wrote a history of the Plymouth Separatists, whom he called "Pilgrims." Part of his original text follows on the left. The text on the right has been edited into modern English.

Old English

1620

I shall a litle returne backe and begine with a **combination** made by them before they came ashore, being ye first foundation of their govermente in this place. . . .

The forme was as followeth.

In ye name of God, Amen. We whose names are underwriten, the loyall subjects of our dread **soveraigne Lord**, King James, . . . haveing **undertaken**, for ye glorie of God, and advancemente of ye Christian faith, and honour of our king & countrie, a voyage to plant

combination/ compact: agreement

soveraigne Lord/ sovereign lord: supreme ruler

undertaken: begun

Modern English

1620

Before the people came ashore they made a **compact**, the first foundation of their government in New England. . . . The form of their compact was as follows:

In the name of God, Amen. We whose names are underwritten, loyal subjects of our dread **sovereign lord**, King James, . . . having **undertaken**, for the Glory of God and advancement of the Christian Faith, and honor of our King and Country, a voyage to plant the first colony in the

1620

1620 Pilgrims sign the Mayflower Compact before landing at Plymouth.

1621 William Bradford becomes governor of Plymouth.

Old English	**Modern English**

ye first colonie in ye Northerne parts of Virginia, doe by these presents solemnly & **mutualy** in ye presence of God, and one of another, **covenant** & combine our selves togeather into a **civill body politick**, for our better ordering & preservation & **furtherance** of ye ends aforesaid; and by vertue hearof to **enacte, constitute, and frame** such just & equall lawes, ordinances, acts, constitutions, & offices, from time to time, as shall be thought most meete & convenient for ye generall good of ye Colonie, unto which we promise all due submission and obedience. In witnes wherof we have hereunder **subscribed** our names at Cap-Codd ye 11. of November, . . . 1620.

After this they chose, or rather confirmed, M^r. John Carver . . . their Governour for that year. . . .

But hear I cannot but stay and make a pause, and stand half amased at this poore peoples presente condition; and so I thinke will the reader too, when he well considers ye same. Being thus passed ye vast ocean, and a sea of troubles before in their preparation . . . they had now no freinds to wellcome them, nor inns to entertaine or refresh their weather-beaten bodys, no houses or much less townes to repaire too, to seeke for succoure. . . . And for ye season it was winter, and they that know ye winters of ye cuntrie know them to be sharp & violent, & subjecte to cruell & feirce stormes,

---

northern parts of Virginia, do by this document solemnly and **mutually** in the presence of God, and one another, **covenant** and combine ourselves together into a **civil body politic**, for our better ordering and preservation and **furtherance** of the ends aforesaid; and by virtue of this document **enact, constitute, and frame** such just and equal laws, ordinances, acts, constitutions and offices, from time to time, as shall be thought right for the general good of the colony, unto which we promise all due submission and obedience. In witness we have hereunder **subscribed** our names at Cape Cod the eleventh of November, . . . 1620 A.D.

After the compact was signed, they chose, or rather confirmed, Mr. John Carver their governor for the year. . . .

Here I cannot help making a pause and stand half amazed at this poor people's present condition. So I think the reader will too when he considers their state. Having passed over the vast ocean, and a sea of troubles in preparation for the voyage, they had now no friends to welcome them, nor inns to entertain or refresh their weather-beaten bodies, no houses, or much less towns, to go to, to seek help. . . . For the season, it was winter. Those who know New England winters know them to be sharp and violent, and subject to cruel and fierce storms. It is

mutualy/mutually: together

covenant: agree

civill body politick/ civil body politic: government

furtherance: helping to move forward

enacte/enact, constitute, and frame: draw up and make into law

subscribed: signed

1647

1630 – 47 William Bradford writes his history, *Of Plimoth Plantation*.

After exploring the coast of Cape Cod, the Pilgrims chose to settle in an area with a good harbor and fresh water. They stepped ashore at Plymouth Rock on December 21, 1620.

Old English

deangerous to travill to known places, much more to serch an unknown coast. Besids, what could they see but a hidious & desolate wildernes, full of wild beasts & willd men? and what **multituds** ther might be of them they knew not. . . . And yᵉ whole countrie, full of woods & thickets, represented a wild & savage heiw. If they looked behind them, ther was yᵉ mighty ocean which they had passed, and was now as a maine barr & goulfe to seperate them from all yᵉ civill parts of yᵉ world. If it be said they had a ship to sucour them, it is trew; but what heard they daly from yᵉ mʳ. & company? but yᵉ with speede they should looke out a place with their **shallop**, wher they would be at some near distance; for yᵉ season was shuch as he would not stirr from thence till a safe harbor was discovered by them wher they would be, and he might goe

Modern English

dangerous to travel to known places, much more to search an unknown coast.

Besides, what could they see but a frightening and lonely wilderness, full of wild beasts and wild men? What **multitudes** there might be of them, they knew not. . . . The whole country, full of woods and thickets, had a wild and savage look. If they looked behind them, there was the mighty ocean which they had passed. It now stood as a main bar and gulf to separate them from all the civilized parts of the world.

If it be said they had a ship to aid them, it is true. But what heard they daily from the master and crew? That they should take the **shallop** and with speed seek out a place to settle, not too far away. For the season was such that the master would not stir till a safe harbor was discovered by them where they wanted to be set

Old English	**Modern English**	

Old English

without danger; and that victells consumed apace, but he must & would keepe sufficient for them selves & their returne. Yea, it was muttered by some, that if they gott not a place in time, they would turne **them** & their goods ashore & leave them. . . . It is true, indeed, ye affections & love of their **brethren** at **Leyden** was cordiall & entire towards them, but they had litle power to help them, or them selves; and how ye case stode betweene them & ye marchants at their coming away, hath allready been declared. What could now sustaine them but ye spirite of God & his grace?

Modern English

ashore, which he might enter without danger. Also, the food supply was being all eaten up, but he must and would keep enough for the return trip. Some of the crew even muttered that if they did not get a place in time, they would put **them** and their goods ashore and leave them. . . . Indeed, it is true that they had the love of their **brethren** in **Leyden**, but those left behind had little power to help, or even help themselves. The way things stood with the merchants at their coming away from England was not too promising. What could sustain them but the spirit of God and His grace?

them: the colonists

brethren: members of the same religious group

Leyden: city in the Netherlands. The Separatists lived there for 11 years before they sailed to America in 1620.

The Pilgrims were not ready for their first winter in Plymouth. They had no shelters to protect them from the cold. More than half died from starvation and disease.

William Bradford was a strong governor for over 30 years. He helped the Pilgrims survive drought, hunger, sickness, and problems with the Native Americans. Bradford died in 1657 at the age of 67. He was buried on a hill near Plymouth. Today his book is the most important source we have for learning about the Pilgrims of Plymouth.

Old English version: From *Bradford's History "Of Plimouth Plantation* (Boston: Wright & Potter Printing Co., 1901), pp. 94–96, 109, 110. Courtesy of the State Library of Massachusetts.

Modern English version: From *Pilgrim Courage*, pp. 26–30, adapted and edited by E. Brooks Smith and Robert Meredith. Copyright © 1962 by Edric B. Smith, Jr. and Robert K. Meredith. Reprinted by permission of Little, Brown and Company.

Letter From New England

John Winthrop

John Winthrop was a lawyer, skilled speaker, and a strong leader. He governed the Massachusetts Bay Colony for nearly 20 years.

The Puritans were English people who were not happy with the Church of England. Many Puritans went to the New World to set up their own church. John Winthrop led the nearly 1,000 Puritans who founded Massachusetts Bay Colony in 1630. After he arrived, he wrote the following letter to his wife. He told her what she must bring when she set out on her journey to their new home.

provisions: supplies of food

bestowed: stored

boatswain: officer in charge of the hull of the ship

quartermasters: officers in charge of supplies on a ship

Charlton in N:[ew] England
July 23, 1630

My dear wife:
   . . . Be sure to be warm clothed and to have store of fresh **provisions:** meal, eggs put up in salt or ground malt, butter, oatmeal, peas, and fruits, and a large, strong chest or two, well locked, to keep these provisions in, and be sure they be **bestowed** in the ship where they may be readily come by, which the **boatswain** will see to and the **quartermasters**, if they be rewarded beforehand. But for these things my son will take care. Be sure to have ready at sea

1620

1620 Plymouth Colony is founded by the Pilgrims.

two or three skillets of several sizes, a large frying pan, a small stewing pan, and **a case to boil a pudding in**, store of linen for use at sea, and **sack** to bestow among the sailors, some drinking vessels, and pewter and other vessels, and for **physic** you shall need no other but a pound of Doctor Wrighte's *Electarium lenitium*, and his direction to use it, a gallon of juice of **scurvy grass** to drink a little, five or six mornings, together with some **saltpeter** dissolved in it, and a little grated or sliced nutmeg.

Thou must be sure to bring no more company than so many as shall have full provision for a year and a half, for though the earth here be very fertile, yet there must be time and means to raise it. If we have corn enough we may live plentifully. . . .

The Lord will in due time let us see the faces of each other again to our great comfort. Now the Lord in mercy bless, guide, and support thee. I kiss and embrace thee, my dear wife. I kiss and bless you all, my dear children, Forth, Mary, Dean, Sam, and **the other**. The Lord keep you all and work His true fear in your hearts. . . .

Remember to come well furnished with linen, woolen, some more bedding, brass, pewter, leather bottles, drinking horns, etc. Let my son provide twelve axes of several sorts of the **Braintree smith** or some other prime workman, whatever they cost, and some **augers** great and small, and many other necessaries which I can't now think of, as candle, soap, and store of beef **suet**, etc. Once again, farewell, my dear wife.

Thy faithful husband,
Jo: Winthrop.

a case to boil a pudding in: a bag, probably of animal skin, used to boil unsweetened pudding

sack: wine

physic: medicine

Electarium lenitium: a special drink made by Winthrop's doctor

scurvy grass: a green vegetable high in vitamin C

saltpeter: potassium

the other: Winthrop's newborn child. He did not yet know it was a girl.

Braintree smith: metal craftsperson in the town of Braintree, England

augers: tools for boring holes, as in wood

suet: animal fat used for cooking and making soap and candles

Massachusetts Bay Colony grew quickly. The colonists wrote to friends and family in England. They told about the freedom and new life they enjoyed in the New World. More and more people came. By 1640 more than 15,000 new settlers had come to Massachusetts Bay. John Winthrop served as governor of the colony almost continuously from its founding in 1630 until his death in 1649.

From Everett Emerson (ed.), *Letters From New England* (Amherst, Mass.: The University of Massachusetts Press, 1976), pp. 46–47. Reprinted by permission of the Massachusetts Historical Society.

1630

1629 The Puritans elect John Winthrop their governor before setting sail.

1630 The Puritans found Massachusetts Bay Colony.

Colonial Wit and Wisdom

“ Little Strokes, Fell great Oaks. ”

Benjamin Franklin

Benjamin Franklin was a man of many talents. In this portrait he is shown with one of his inventions—the lightning rod.

almanac: yearly book with useful information on weather, farming, and other topics arranged by the calendar

Benjamin Franklin wrote and published *Poor Richard's Almanack* for 25 years. In his **almanac** he provided helpful information. He also printed poems and jokes. And he gave advice in short, thoughtful sentences. Each almanac began with a letter from Richard Saunders. "Poor Richard" was a character made up by Franklin. The letters and sayings that follow are from different years of the almanac. ∾

1733

Favour, Almanacks, View: In colonial times nouns were often capitalized. Also, spelling and punctuation rules were not strict.

shift of tow: loose-fitting dress of fabric made from spinning yarn or twine

Courteous Reader,

I might in this place attempt to gain thy **Favour,** by declaring that I write **Almanacks** with no other **View** than that of the publick Good; but in this I should not be sincere. . . . The plain Truth of the Matter is, I am excessive poor, and my Wife, good Woman, is, I tell her, excessive proud; she cannot bear, she says, to sit spinning in her **Shift of Tow**, while I do nothing but gaze at the Stars; and has threatned more than once to burn all my Books and Rattling-Traps (as she calls my Instruments) if I do not make some profitable Use of them for the good of my Family. The Printer has offer'd me some considerable share of the Profits, and I have thus begun to comply with my Dame's desire. . . .

Friend and Servant
R. Saunders.

24

❦ Great Talkers, little Doers.

❦ Eat to live, and not live to eat.

❦ He that lies down with Dogs, shall rise up with fleas.

1734

Courteous Readers,
Your kind and charitable Assistance last Year, in purchasing so large an **Impression** of my Almanacks, has made my **Circumstances** much more easy in the World, and requires my grateful Acknowledgment. My Wife has been **enabled** to get a Pot of her own, and is no longer **oblig'd** to borrow one from a Neighbour; nor have we ever since been without something of our own to put in it. . . . Accept my hearty Thanks therefor, and my sincere Wishes for your Health and Prosperity.

Your poor Friend and Servant,
R. Saunders.

❦ No man e'er was glorious, who was not **laborious**.

❦ In success be moderate.

❦ Take this remark from *Richard* poor and **lame**,
Whate'er's begun in anger ends in shame.

❦ Hope of gain Lessens pain.

❦ Be neither silly, nor cunning, but wise.

❦ All things are cheap to the saving, **dear** to the wasteful.

❦ Do good to thy Friend to keep him, to thy enemy to gain him.

1735

❦ Early to bed and early to rise, makes a man healthy wealthy and wise.

1736

❦ Fish & Visitors stink in 3 days.

❦ Don't throw stones at your neighbours, if your own windows are glass.

impression: number of copies printed at one time

circumstances: the way in which a person lives, especially with regard to money

enabled: able to afford

oblig'd: forced

laborious: hard-working

lame: crippled

dear: expensive

1733

1729　Franklin begins publishing *The Pennsylvania Gazette,* a successful newspaper.

1733　Franklin publishes the first edition of *Poor Richard's Almanack.*

Franklin's almanacs were filled with advice as well as information.

1738

preface: introduction

***Preface** by Mistress Saunders*
Dear Readers,

My good Man set out last Week for *Potowmack*, to visit an old **Stargazer** of his Acquaintance. . . . He left the Copy of his Almanack seal'd up, and bid me send it to the Press. I suspected something, and therefore as soon as he was gone, I open'd it. . . . He had put into his Preface, that his Wife *Bridget*—was **this, and that, and t'other**. . . . In short, I thought the Preface was not worth a printing, and so I fairly scratch'd it all out, and I believe you'll like our Almanack never the worse for it. . . .

stargazer: astronomer

this, and that, and t'other: Richard had made fun of certain sides of his wife's personality.

Your loving friend,
Bridget Saunders

deceiv'd: fooled

🍂 Who has **deceiv'd** thee so oft as thy self?

🍂 Wish not so much to live long as to live well.

1740

foe: enemy

🍂 An open **Foe** may prove a curse; But a pretended friend is worse.

🍂 Promises may get thee Friends, but Nonperformance will turn them into Enemies.

1741

🍂 If you would keep your Secret from an enemy, tell it not to a friend.

sluggard: lazy person

🍂 Up, **Sluggard**, and waste not life; in the grave will be sleeping enough.

🍂 Quarrels never could last long, If on one side only lay the wrong.

1744

❧ Tart Words make no Friends: a spoonful of honey
will catch more flies than a Gallon of Vinegar.

❧ Make haste slowly.

❧ A true Friend is the best Possession.

1750

. . . This, kind Reader, is my seventeenth Labour of the Kind. Thro'
thy continued Good-will, they have procur'd me, if no **Bays**, at least
Pence; and the latter is perhaps the better of the two; since 'tis not improb-
able that a Man may receive more solid Satisfaction from *Pudding*, while
he is *living*, than from *Praise*, after he is *dead*. . . .

Thy obliged Friend,
R. Saunders.

bays: a crown of leaves from the bay tree; a symbol of honor

pence: money

❧ Little Strokes, Fell great Oaks.

❧ Genius without Education is like Silver in the Mine.

This engraving appeared in an 1859 copy of *Poor Richard's Illustrated*.

Almanacs were important to the colonists. They contained many kinds of
information. Many almanacs came out each year. But Franklin's was the
favorite. His wise and funny sayings were popular with everyone. People
enjoyed *Poor Richard's Almanack* so much that they bought 10,000 copies
each year. Franklin's sayings are still quoted today.

Text reprinted from *Benjamin Franklin, Writings*, published by the Library of America,
1987, by permission.

FIGHTING FOR FREEDOM

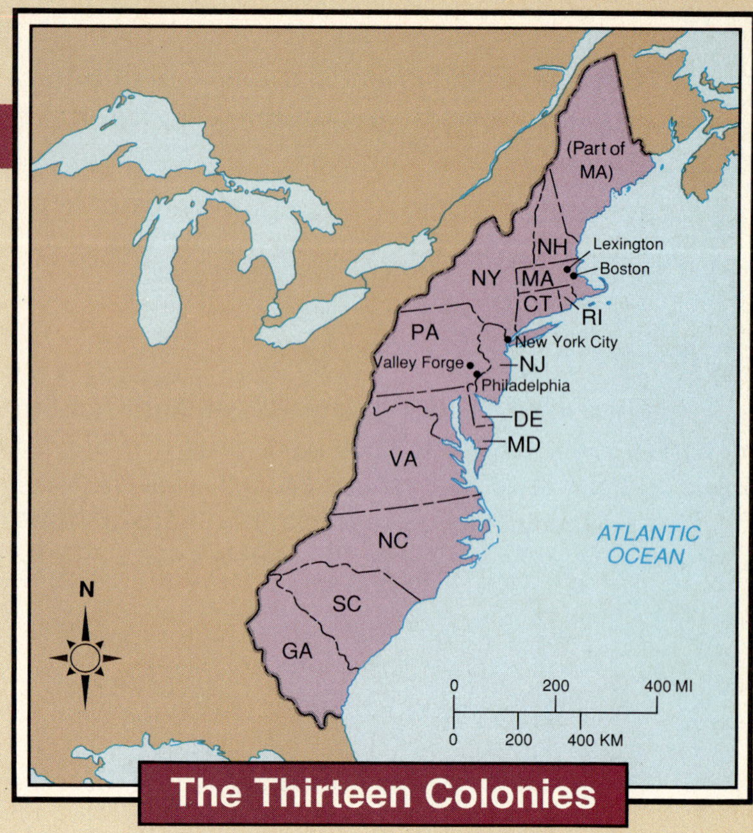

The Thirteen Colonies

French and Indian War: war in the American colonies in which France and Great Britain fought for control of the Ohio River valley (1754–1763)

Parliament: lawmaking body of Great Britain

militia: volunteers who could be called on to fight in an emergency

America fought the Revolutionary War to gain freedom from British rule. Most early colonists were happy to be British citizens. They were also happy that the British government left them alone.

Beginning in 1763 Great Britain began to gain more control over the colonies. The **French and Indian War** left Great Britain with a huge debt. To help raise money, the British government taxed goods sent to the colonies from Great Britain. With each new tax the colonists grew more angry.

The colonists said the taxes were unfair because the colonies could not vote for the British **Parliament**. As things got worse, a growing number of people began to argue for independence. They called themselves Patriots. The British placed troops in many towns to keep order. Groups of Patriots armed themselves in response. Near Boston on April 19, 1775, fighting broke out between colonial **militia** and British troops. More small battles

1765   1770

■ **1767** **British Parliament passes the Townshend Acts which tax imported goods such as tea.**

followed. By July 2, 1776, the colonies had declared their independence. And the war was under way.

The Patriots were poorly prepared for war. Most of their soldiers were untrained. The British won more victories at first. In early 1777 the British forced American troops to make a long retreat from New York to Philadelphia. General George Washington's troops had to camp through the winter at nearby Valley Forge. Many soldiers died from hunger, cold, and sickness. Thousands of other American soldiers ran away because of the terrible conditions. Only the most loyal soldiers remained.

In the same year, however, the Americans defeated the British at Saratoga, New York. This victory made the French believe that the Americans could win the war. France entered the war on the side of the colonists. Without French help, the Patriots would probably not have won the war.

The first shot of the Revolutionary War was fired at the Battle of Lexington in Massachusetts. The war for independence had begun.

Each reading in this unit provides a glimpse of Patriot life during the Revolutionary War.

- The songs **"Revolutionary Tea"** and **"Yankee Doodle"** express the patriotic spirit of the colonists.
- In letters to her husband John, **Abigail Adams** writes about her political views and events at home.
- A Connecticut soldier, **James Sullivan Martin**, tells how American troops suffered at Valley Forge.

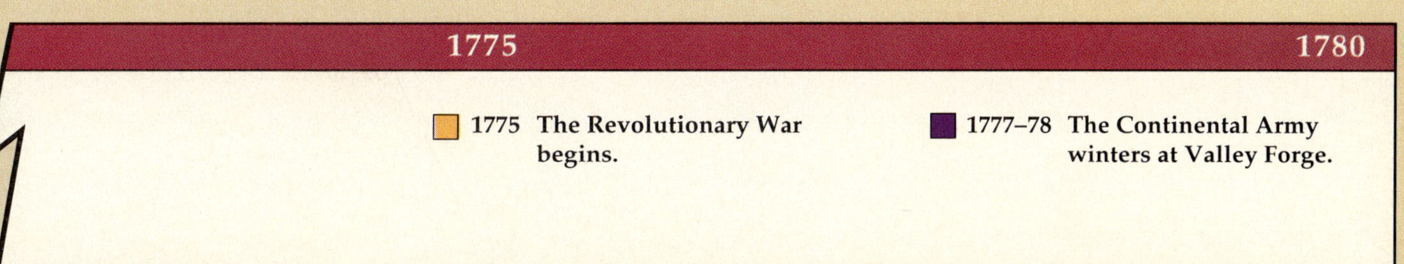

Songs of the Patriots

Dressed as Mohawks, colonists boarded British ships and tossed 342 chests of tea into the harbor.

News spread slowly in colonial America. Sometimes news was carried in the form of a song. Songs were easy to learn and remember, and singing them was fun. Most authors wrote their verses to a well-known melody. Texts were printed quickly and cheaply on a single large sheet of paper called a broadside. Broadsides were sold on the street and in the marketplace. Soon all of the townspeople heard the song and learned about the news.

The following songs are examples of broadsides. "Revolutionary Tea" tells how the colonists felt about the tea tax. "Yankee Doodle" exists in many versions. The earliest set of verses was sung by the British to poke fun at the colonial soldiers. But the Americans liked the song and made it their own. Edward Bangs, a Patriot who fought at Lexington, wrote this revised version of "Yankee Doodle." It became very popular during the Revolutionary War.

Colonists ready to fight at a minute's notice were called minutemen. They left their jobs as shopkeepers, teachers, and farmers to take on the British army.

1767

1767 The Townshend Acts raise the taxes on imported goods such as tea, glass, lead, and paint.

1773 A group of Patriots dump 342 chests of British-owned tea (worth about $90,000) into Boston Harbor.

1775 Edward Bangs witnesses the Battle of Lexington.

Revolutionary Tea

contented: happy

pence: pennies

❧2

"Now mother, dear mother," the
    daughter replied,
"I shan't do the thing that you **ax;**
I'm willing to pay a fair price for
    the tea,
But never the three penny tax."
"You shall," **quoth** the mother,
    and reddened with rage,
"For you're my own daughter,
    you see,
And sure 'tis quite proper the
    daughter should pay
Her mother a tax on her tea,
Her mother a tax on her tea."

❧3

And so the old lady her servant
    called up,
And packed off a **budget** of tea;
And eager for three pence a
    pound, she put in
Enough for a large family.

She ordered her servants to bring
    home the tax,
Declaring her child should obey,
Or old as she was, and almost
    woman grown,
She'd half whip her life away,
She'd half whip her life away.

❧4

The tea was **conveyed** to the
    daughter's door,
All down by the ocean's side;
And the bouncing girl poured out
    every pound
In the **dark and boiling tide**.
And then she called out to the
    Island Queen,
"Oh, mother, dear mother,"
    quoth she,
"Your tea you may have when
    'tis **steeped** enough,
But never a tax from me,
But never a tax from me."

ax: (ask)

quoth: said

budget: load

conveyed: carried

*dark and boiling
tide:* Boston Harbor

steeped: soaked in
liquid to get the
flavor

1781 Washington's army and the French fleet force the British to surrender at Yorktown, Virginia.	**1783** America and Great Britain sign the Treaty of Paris, ending the Revolutionary War.

1783

Yankee Doodle

Doodle: do-little;
a lazy person

macaroni:
fashionable

dandy: a person
who loves fancy
clothes

camp: a British
camp

hasty puddin':
(hasty pudding)
a mush made of flour
or oatmeal

Squire: title for an
English country
gentleman

keg: a small barrel

stallion: horse

swamping gun:
large gun on wheels
that is moved from
battle to battle

hooked it off: ran
away

2
Father and I went down to **camp**,
Along with Captain Good'in,
And there we saw the men and
    boys
As thick as **hasty puddin'**.
Chorus

3
And there we saw a thousand men
As rich as **Squire** David;
And what they wasted ev'ry day,
I wish it could be saved.
Chorus

4
And there I saw a little **keg,**
Its head all made of leather,
They knocked on it with little
    sticks
To call the folks together.
Chorus

5
And there was Captain
    Washington
Upon a slapping **stallion,**
A-giving orders to his men—
I guess there was a million.
Chorus

6
And there I saw a **swamping gun**,
Large as a log of maple,
Upon a mighty little cart—
A load for father's cattle.
Chorus

7
And every time they fired it off,
It took a horn of powder;
It made a noise like father's gun,
Only a nation louder!
Chorus

8
The troopers, too, would gallop up
And fire right in our faces;
It scared me almost half to death
To see them run such races.
Chorus

9
It scared me so I **hooked it off**,
Nor stopped, as I remember,
Nor turned about till I got home,
Locked up in mother's chamber.
Chorus

In *The Spirit of '76*, painted by Archibald Willard in 1875, a fife player and drummers bravely lead the Americans into battle.

Songs such as ''Yankee Doodle'' and ''Revolutionary Tea'' help us understand events from the past. They also show how people felt at the time. Like many songs about special events in history, ''Revolutionary Tea'' is rarely sung today. It is said that ''Yankee Doodle'' was sung by the colonials when the British surrendered at Yorktown. Americans still sing this merry song in many versions.

From *Annals of America*, vol. 2 (Chicago: Encyclopedia Britannica, 1976), p. 245. Music from *Father Kemp's Old Folks' Concert Tunes* (Oliver Ditson Co., 1889) as it appeared in *Songs of Independence*, p. 55, by Irwin Silber, published by Stackpole Books. Copyright © 1973.

From Edward Bangs, *Steven Kellogg's Yankee Doodle* (New York: Four Winds Press, 1976). Musical arrangement from Wilson et al., *Growing with Music*, Related Arts Edition, Book 3, p. 92. (Englewood Cliffs, NJ: Prentice-Hall, Inc. © 1970).

From Abigail to John

Abigail Adams

Abigail Adams wrote many letters to her husband John while he was at the First Continental Congress in Philadelphia.

formidable:
dreadful

Mr. Welds:
a minister

sent of an express:
sent a messenger

sloops: small sailing
ships

cutter: larger sailing
ship

design: plan

Drs.: doctors; a term
of respect

War broke out in April 1775 near Boston. John and Abigail Adams lived close by in Braintree. Abigail looked after the farm and family. John was in Philadelphia at the First Continental Congress. Husband and wife wrote each other often. In her letters Abigail told of events near their hometown. She also expressed her ideas about American independence. Her writing reflects the style of the time. Spelling, punctuation, and capitalization rules in the 1700s were not strict.

24 May Braintree 1775
Suppose you have had a **formidable** account of the alarm we had last Sunday morning. When I rose about six oclock I was told that the Drums had been some time beating and that 3 allarm Guns were fired, that Weymouth Bell had been ringing, and **Mr. Welds** was then ringing. I immediatly **sent of an express** to know the occasion, and found the whole Town in confusion. 3 **Sloops** and one **cutter** had come out, and droped anchor just below Great Hill. It was difficult to tell their **design**, some supposed they were comeing to Germantown others to Weymouth. People women children from the Iron Works flocking down this Way— every woman and child above or from below my Fathers. My Fathers family flying, the **Drs.** in great distress, as you may well immagine for my Aunt had her Bed thrown into a cart, into which she got herself, and orderd the boy

1764	
1764 Abigail Smith marries John Adams.	**1774** John Adams attends the First Continental Congress. Abigail takes charge of their farm.

to drive her **of** to Bridgwater which he did. The report was to them, that 300 hundred had landed, and were upon their march into Town. The allarm flew [like] lightning, and men from all parts came flocking down till 2000 were collected—but it seems their **expidition** was to Grape Island for *Levet's* hay. . . . We expect soon to be in continual alarms, till something decisive takes place. We wait with longing Expectation in hopes to hear the best accounts from you with regard to union and harmony **&c**. We rejoice greatly on the Arival of **Doctor Franklin**, as he must certainly be able to inform you very perticuliarly of the situation of affairs in England. I wish you would [write] if you can get time; be as perticuliar as you *may*, when you write—every one here abouts come[s] to me to hear what accounts I have. . . .

November 27 1775

. . . I wish I knew what mighty things were **fabricating**. If a form of Goverment is to be established here what one will be **assumed**? Will it be left to our assemblies to chuse one? and will not many men have many minds? and shall we not run into **Dissentions** among ourselves?

I am more and more convinced that Man is a dangerous creature, and that power whether **vested in** many or a few is ever grasping, and like the grave cries give, give. The great fish swallow up the small, and he who is most strenuous for the Rights of the people, when vested with power, is as eager after the **perogatives** of Goverment. You tell me of degrees of perfection to which **Humane** Nature is capable of arriving, and I believe it, but at the same time **lament** that our admiration should

of: (off)

expidition: (expedition) journey

Levet's: probably a neighbor's

&c.: and so on

Doctor Franklin: Benjamin Franklin

fabricating: in the making

assumed: taken on

dissentions: disagreements

vested in: held by

perogatives: (prerogatives) privileges

humane: (human)

lament: feel sadness

John Adams (left of table) was one of five men chosen to write the Declaration of Independence. In this painting by John Trumbull the committee presents the finished declaration to Congress.

1775 The Revolutionary War begins.

1776 John Adams signs the Declaration of Independence.

1783 The Adamses live in Europe while John is American ambassador.

arise from the **scarcity of the instances**.

The Building up a Great Empire, which was only hinted at by my **correspondent** may now I suppose be realized even by the unbelievers. Yet will not ten thousand Difficulties arise in the formation of it? The **Reigns** of Goverment have been so long **slakned**, that I fear the people will not quietly submit to those restraints which are necessary for the peace, and security, of the community; if we seperate from Brittain, what Code of Laws will be established. How shall we be governd so as to retain our Liberties? Can any goverment be free which is not **adminstred** by general stated Laws? Who shall frame these Laws? Who will give them force and energy? Tis true your Resolution[s] as a **Body** have **heithertoo** had the force of Laws. But will they continue to have?

Braintree March 31 1776

. . . I long to hear that you have declared an independancy— and by the way in the new Code of Laws which I suppose it will be necessary for you to make I desire you would Remember the Ladies, and be more generous and favour- able to them than your ancestors. Do not put such unlimited power into the hands of the Husbands. Remember all Men would be **tyrants** if they could. If perticuliar care and attention is not paid to the Laidies we are determined to **foment** a Rebelion, and will not hold ourselves bound by any Laws in which we have no voice, or Representation.

That your Sex are Naturally Tyrannical is a Truth so thoroughly established as to admit of no dispute, but such of you as wish to

be happy willingly give up the harsh title of Master for the more tender and endearing one of Friend. Why then, not put it out of the power of the vicious and the Lawless to use us with cruelty and indignity **with impunity**. Men of Sense in all Ages **abhor** those customs which treat us only as the **vassals** of your Sex. Regard us then as Beings placed by **providence** under your protection and in immitation of the **Supreem Being** make use of that power only for our happiness.

July 21 1776 Boston

. . . Last Thursday after hearing a very Good Sermon I went with the **Multitude** into Kings Street to hear the proclamation for inde- pendance read and proclamed. . . . As soon as **he** ended, the cry from the **Belcona**, was God Save our American States and then 3 cheers which **rended** the air, the Bells rang, the **privateers** fired, the forts and Batteries, the cannon were

In this painting by Howard Pyle, George Washington faces his army to hear the reading of the Declaration of Independence in 1776.

discharged, the **platoons** followed and every face appeard joyfull. **Mr. Bowdoin** then gave a Sentiment, Stability and **perpetuity** to American independance. After dinner the **kings arms** were taken down from the State House and every **vestage** of him from every place in which it appeard and burnt in King Street. Thus ends royall Authority in this State, and all the people shall say Amen. . . .

Boston October 25 1777
Saturday Evening

The joyfull News of the Surrender of **General Burgoin** and all his Army to our Victorious Troops prompted me to take a ride this afternoon with my daughter to Town to join to morrow with my Friends in thanksgiving and praise to the Supreem Being who hath so remarkably deliverd our Enimies into our Hands. . . .

This day dearest of Friends compleats 13 years since we were **solemly** united in wedlock; 3 years of the time we have been cruelly seperated. I have patiently as I could endured it with the Belief that you were serving your Country, and **rendering** your fellow creatures essential Benefits. . . .

Adieu dearest of Friends adieu.

Liberty bells rang out across the colonies as Americans fought for their independence from Great Britain.

Abigail and John wrote nearly 300 letters to each other between 1774 and 1783. Abigail's letters have a clear and pleasant style. They contain comments and advice on political matters. They also give news about friends and family. John Adams became president of the United States in 1797. The Adamses were the first family to live in the White House.

Reprinted by permission of the publishers from *Adams Family Correspondence*, L. H. Butterfield, ed. Cambridge, Mass.: The Belknap Press of Harvard University Press, Copyright © 1963 by the Massachusetts Historical Society. Excerpts from pp. 56, 204–5, 328–30, 358–59, 369–70.

---

platoons: groups of soldiers

Mr. Bowdoin: probably a townsperson

perpetuity: health forever

kings arms: the coat of arms of George III, a symbol of his power

vestage: (vestige) trace

General Burgoin: (Burgoyne) British General Burgoyne's defeat at Saratoga, New York, was an important victory for the Americans.

solemly: (solemnly) with dignity

rendering: giving

adieu: French for farewell (God be with you)

Winter of Despair

" The army was now not only starved but naked. . . . "

James Sullivan Martin

Soldiers huddled around fires to keep warm during the long, cold winter at Valley Forge.

In December 1777 General George Washington set up camp at Valley Forge near Philadelphia, Pennsylvania. His 10,000 soldiers were tired. They lacked food, water, clothing, and proper shelter. Thousands died from sickness and exposure to the cold. Thousands more, losing hope, deserted. A soldier describes the horrid conditions at Valley Forge. ∞

rioted in its glory: was out of control

Commissary's quarters: place where food and supplies are stored

hocks: a poor cut of meat, from just above the hoof

messmates: soldiers who usually eat together

purloined: stole

obliged: forced

destitute of: without

Soon after the British had quit their position on Chestnut-hill, we left this place, and after marching and countermarching back and forward some days, . . . we at last settled down at a place called ''the Gulf''. . . and here we encamped some time, and here we had liked to have encamped forever— for starvation here *rioted* **in its glory**. . . .

As we returned to our camp, we passed by our **Commissary's quarters**; all his stores, consisting of a barrel about two thirds full of **hocks** of fresh beef, stood directly in our way, but there was a senti-nel guarding even that; however, one of my **messmates purloined** a piece of it, four or five pounds perhaps. I was exceeding glad to see him take it; . . . how soon my expectations were blasted! The sentinel saw him have it as soon as I did and **obliged** him to return it to the barrel again. So I had nothing else to do but to go home and make out my supper as usual, upon a leg of nothing and no turnips.

The army was now not only starved but naked; the greatest part were not only shirtless and barefoot, but **destitute of** all other

Sept. 1777		
Sept. 1777 The British occupy Philadelphia.	**Oct. 1777** Washington's troops are defeated at Germantown, Pennsylvania.	**Dec. 1777** Washington and his troops set up camp at Valley Forge.

clothing, especially blankets. I **procured** a small piece of raw cowhide and made myself a pair of **moccasons**, which kept my feet (while they lasted) from the frozen ground, although, as I well remember, the hard edges so **galled** my **ancles**, while on a march, that it was with much difficulty and pain that I could wear them afterwards; but the only **alternative** I had was to **endure this inconvenience** or to go barefoot, as hundreds of my companions had to, till they might be tracked by their blood upon the rough frozen ground. But hunger, nakedness and sore shins were not the only difficulties we had at that time to encounter; we had hard duty to perform and little or no strength to perform it with. . . .

We arrived at the Valley Forge in the evening; it was dark; there was no water to be found, and I was **perishing** with thirst. I searched for water till I was weary, and came to my tent without finding any; fatigue and thirst, joined with hunger, almost made me desperate. I felt at that instant as if I would have taken **victuals** or drink from the best friend I had on earth by force. I am not writing **fiction**; all are **sober realities**. Just after I arrived at my tent, two soldiers, whom I did not know, passed by; they had some water in their canteens which they told me they had found a good distance off, but could not direct me to the place as it was very dark. I tried to beg a **draught** of water from them. . . . I persuaded them to sell me a drink for three **pence**, . . . which was every cent of property I could then call my own. . . .

General George Washington reviews his ragged army at Valley Forge after losing Philadelphia to the British.

procured: got

moccasons: (moccasins)

galled: rubbed sore

ancles: (ankles)

alternative: other choice

endure this inconvenience: put up with this hardship

perishing: dying

victuals: food

fiction: untruths

sober realities: serious truths

draught: drink

pence: pennies

The winter spent at Valley Forge was a time of despair. But it was also a turning point. In late winter German officer Baron von Steuben helped Washington train his troops. With the arrival of spring came clothing, food, and troop replacements. In May the news of French aid gave the troops hope. The fight for independence continued.

Excerpt from *The Spirit of 'Seventy-six* by Henry Steele Commager and Richard B. Morris ed., pp. 642–44. Copyright © 1958, 1967, 1975 by Henry Steele Commager and Richard B. Morris. Reprinted by permission of Harper and Row, Publishers, Inc.

May 1778

Feb. 1778 **Baron von Steuben arrives at Valley Forge to help train soldiers.**

May 1778 **News of the French alliance reaches Valley Forge.**

A NEW NATION

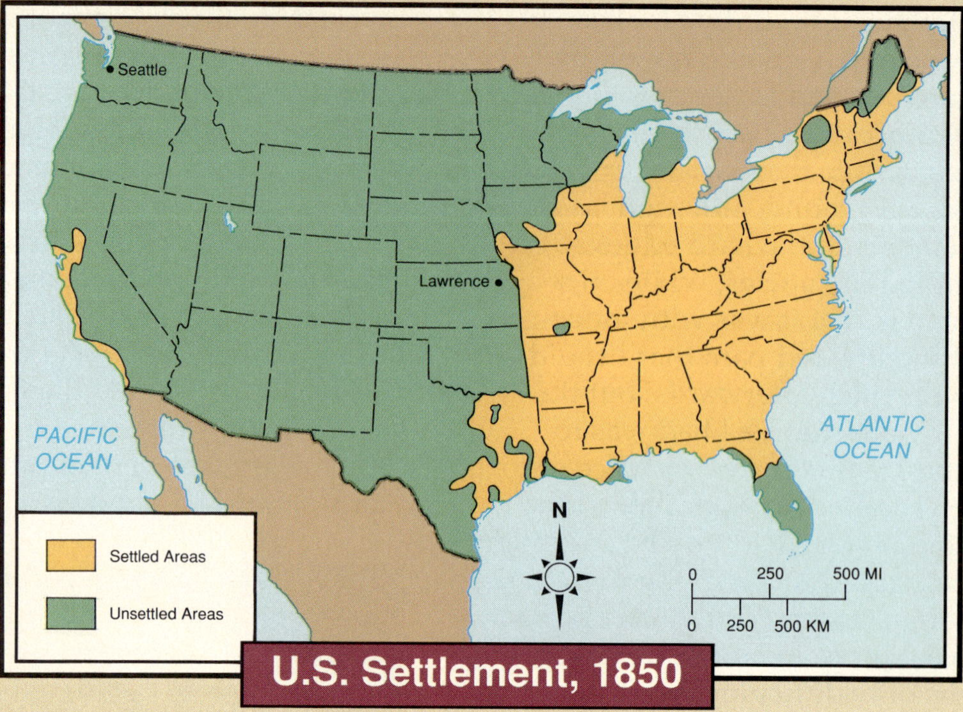

U.S. Settlement, 1850

Gold Rush: a rush of people to an area in California where gold had been found in 1848

reservations: public lands set aside by the government for Native Americans

The century after the Revolutionary War was one of great expansion. After the war the United States got a huge amount of land from the British. In 1803 it bought land from the French. In 1848 it won land from the Spanish. By the 1850s United States territory stretched from coast to coast.

This new land drew pioneers westward by the thousands. Some went by covered wagon and boat. Others struggled on foot and on horseback. They faced great dangers. Many went west to make a better life for themselves. Others traveled in search of adventure and wealth. The **Gold Rush** which began in 1848 pulled thousands to California. The flow of people to the West would continue for several decades.

This westward movement nearly destroyed the Native Americans. Wars between Native Americans and settlers moving west occurred over land disputes. The United States government forced the Native Americans to give up their homelands. It placed them on **reservations**. Many were put on land that was useless or strange to them. Many Native Americans starved to death. Others died from diseases brought by white people. Before 1500 Native

1855	1856	1857

1855 **The U.S. government signs peace treaties with several Northwest tribes. Tribes are moved to reservations.**

1857 **The Carpenters begin their journey to California.**

Americans in North America numbered over one million. By 1900 fewer than 350,000 remained.

Black slaves also suffered during this time of expansion. Slaves had been brought to America since the 1600s. By the early 1800s many southern states depended on slave labor. Most slaves worked on large **plantations**. Many owners were cruel to their slaves. People began to speak out against slavery. They thought that slavery had no place in a country built on democracy and freedom. The issue of slavery would divide the nation.

A flood of pioneers in covered wagons crossed the Great Plains in search of new land and wealth.

In this unit three people report their personal challenges and changes in the new nation.

- **Chief Seattle** gives a moving speech about the sad decline of Native Americans.
- In her journal a young pioneer named **Helen Carpenter** describes her trip west.
- Former slave **Harriet Jacobs** describes the misery of slave life in her autobiography.

1858	1859	1860

1860 The slave population in America totals about 4 million.

Chief Seattle Speaks

Chief Seattle

Chief Seattle was the leader of several Native American tribes in the Washington Territory.

In the 1840s thousands of settlers came to the Northwest. They hoped to find rich farmland or gold. They took over much of the land that Native Americans had lived on for thousands of years. Fighting often broke out between the two groups. In 1855 United States officials and Native American leaders met to sign peace treaties. The Native Americans were persuaded to give up their lands and move to reservations. Chief Seattle, leader of many tribes in the Northwest, made this speech to the governor of the Washington Territory.

great chief: U.S. President Franklin Pierce

resemble: look like

presume: suppose or assume

extensive: large; far-reaching

My words are like the stars that never change. Whatever Seattle says the **great chief** at Washington can rely upon with as much certainty as he can upon the return of the sun or the seasons. The White Chief says that Big Chief at Washington sends us greetings of friendship and good will. This is kind of him for we know he has little need of our friendship in return. His people are many. They are like the grass that covers vast prairies. My people are few. They **resemble** the scattering trees of a storm-swept plain. The Great—and I **presume**—good White Chief sends us word that he wishes to buy our lands but is willing to allow us enough to live comfortably. This indeed appears just, even generous, for the Red Man no longer has rights that he need respect, and the offer may be wise also, as we are no longer in need of an **extensive** country.

There was a time when our people covered the land as the waves of a wind-ruffled sea cover

1848 Gold is discovered in California. Settlers moving west dispute with Native Americans over land.

1853 The U.S. Congress creates the Washington Territory.

1856 War breaks out in the Northwest between settlers and Native Americans. U.S. troops are called in.

its shell-paved floor, but that time long since passed away with the greatness of tribes that are now but a **mournful** memory. I will not **dwell on**, nor mourn over, our **untimely decay**, nor **reproach** my pale face brothers with **hastening** it as we too may have been some-what to blame.

Youth is **impulsive**. When our young men grow angry at some real or imaginary wrong, and **disfigure** their faces with black paint, . . . then they are often cruel . . . and our old men and old women are unable to **restrain** them. Thus it has ever been. Thus it was when the white man first began to push our forefathers westward. But let us hope that the **hostilities** between us may never return. We would have everything to lose and nothing to gain. . . .

Our **good father** at Washington . . . sends us word that if we do as he desires he will protect us. His brave warriors will be to us a **bristling** wall of strength, and his wonderful ships of war will fill our harbors so that our ancient enemies . . . will **cease** to frighten our women, children and old men. Then in reality will he be our father and we his children. But can that ever be? Your God is not our God! Your God loves your people and hates mine. He folds his strong protecting arms lovingly about the pale face and leads him by the hand as a father leads his infant son—but He has **forsaken** His red children—if they are really His. Our God, the Great Spirit, seems also to have forsaken us. Your God makes your people **wax** strong every day. Soon they will fill all the land. Our people are **ebbing** away like a rapidly **receding** tide that will never return. The white man's God can

The Native Americans who lived in the Northwest fished the coastal waters for salmon, cod, and halibut.

mournful: sad and sorrowful

dwell on: go on thinking or talking about for a long time

untimely decay: sudden or early decline. The tribes were decreasing in strength and numbers.

reproach: blame

hastening: hurrying

impulsive: likely to act without thinking

disfigure: change the look of by marking up

restrain: control

hostilities: acts of war

good father: President Pierce

bristling: rigid

cease: stop

forsaken: given up; abandoned

wax: grow

ebbing: fading

receding: falling backward

1877

1877 **The last major Native American uprising in the Northwest ends with the surrender of Chief Joseph.**

Native Americans used cedar bark and wool from mountain goats to make blankets and clothing.

not love our people or He would protect them. They seem to be orphans who can look nowhere for help. How then can we be brothers? . . . No. We are two **distinct** races with separate origins and separate **destinies**. There is little in common between us.

. . . Day and night can not dwell together. The Red Man has ever fled the approach of the White Man as the morning mist flees before the rising sun.

However, your **proposition** seems fair, and I think that my folks will accept it and will retire to the **reservation** you offer them. Then we will dwell apart in peace for the words of the Great White Chief seem to be the voice of Nature speaking to my people out of dense darkness.

It matters little where we pass the **remnant** of our days. They will not be many. The Indian's night promises to be dark. Not a single star of hope **hovers** above his horizon. Sad-voiced winds moan in the distance. Grim **Nemesis** seems to be on the Red Man's trail, and wherever he goes he will hear the approaching footsteps of his **fell** destroyer and prepare to **stolidly** meet his doom, as does the wounded doe that hears the approaching footsteps of the hunter.

A few more moons. A few more winters—and not one of the **descendants** of the mighty **hosts** that once moved over this broad land or lived in happy homes, protected by the Great Spirit, will remain to mourn over the graves of a people—once more powerful and hopeful than yours. But why should I mourn at the untimely fate of my people? Tribe follows tribe, and nation follows nation, like the waves of the sea. It is the order of nature, and regret is useless. Your time of **decay** may be distant—but it will surely come, for even the White Man whose God walked and talked with him as friend with friend, can not be **exempt** from the **common destiny**. We may be brothers after all. We will see.

We will **ponder** your proposition and when we decide we will let you know. But should we accept it, I here and now make this condition—that we will not be denied the privilege without **molestation**, of visiting at any time the tombs of our ancestors, friends and children. Every part of this soil is **sacred**, in the **estimation** of my people. Every hillside, every valley, every plain and grove, has been **hallowed** by some sad or happy event in days long vanished. Even the rocks, which seem to be dumb and dead as they **swelter** in the sun along the silent shore thrill with memories of stirring events connected with the lives of my people, and the very dust upon which you now stand responds more lovingly to their footsteps than to yours, because it is rich with the dust of our ancestors. . . . Our departed braves, fond mothers, glad, happy-hearted maidens, and even the little children who lived here and rejoiced here for a brief season, still love these **somber solitudes**. . . . And when the last Red Man shall have perished, and the memory of my tribe shall have become a myth among the white man, these shores will **swarm** with the invisible dead of my tribe, and when your children's children think themselves alone in the field, the store, the shop, upon the highway, or in the silence of the pathless woods, they will not be alone. In all the earth there is no place dedicated to **solitude**. At night when the streets of your cities and villages are silent and you think them **deserted**, they will **throng** with the returning hosts that once filled them and still love this beautiful land. The White Man will never be alone.

Let him be just and deal kindly with my people, for the dead are not powerless. Dead—I say? There is no death. Only a change of worlds.

sacred: holy

estimation: judgment

hallowed: made holy and respected

swelter: become sweaty from great heat

somber solitudes: quiet and lonely places

swarm: be filled

solitude: being alone

deserted: empty of people

throng: be crowded

Settlers brought their religion with them when they moved west. Many set up Christian schools. Here Catholic priests are shown with their Native American students.

A few months after Chief Seattle signed the treaty, war broke out again. The fighting continued for about three years. Army troops finally defeated the Native Americans. Their numbers decreased from then on. Chief Seattle often helped the white settlers in the area. Thankful settlers named their town Seattle after him. He died in 1866.

Setting Out to Cross the Plains

" All that trouble is over with now, and we are not worrying about what is ahead of us. "

Helen Carpenter

Thousands of settlers joined wagon trains to make the long journey west. Some wagon trains were several miles long.

yoking them up: joining two cattle with a wooden frame around their necks

Lawrence: city in Kansas that was a starting point for many traveling west

dry goods: supplies such as cloth, matches, and medicines, not including food or hardware

spencer waists: close-fitting, waist-length jackets worn by women in the 19th century

jeans: heavy cotton fabric similar to denim

In the 1840s the first large wave of settlers from the East reached the West. In 1848 gold was discovered in California. Gold seekers streamed into California by the tens of thousands. Thousands more were drawn to the rich farmland of the Northwest and mild climate of California. Most made the long, dangerous journey in covered wagons. In her diary Helen Carpenter, a bride of 19, recorded her trip to California in 1857.

May 26, 1857
Ho—for California—at last we are on the way—only seven miles from home (which is to be home no longer) yet we have really started, and with good luck may someday reach the "promised land." The trip has been so long talked of, and the preparations have gone on under so many disadvantages, that to be ready at last, to start, is something of an event.

At least two trips were made down into Missouri for young cattle for the teams. Then came the "breaking" process, which was accomplished by **yoking them up** and putting them "in the swing" between old Smut and Snarley (leaders) and Dave and Start (wheelers). . . . Then there were several trips to **Lawrence** (15 miles) for **dry goods** and food supplies. I got two pairs of shoes, calico for two **spencer waists**, **jeans** for a dress skirt, needles, pins and thread and so forth. In the way of supplies there was flour, sugar, bacon and ham, tea, coffee, crackers, dried herring, a small quantity of corn starch,

1841	
1841 **The Oregon Trail is used by the first large group of settlers.**	**1848** **After a war with Mexico the United States receives California. The Gold Rush begins.**

dried apples that we brought from Indiana, one bottle of pickles, cream of tartar and soda and that about made up the outfit. Not having fresh fruit in the **Territory**, we have no jam or preserves. All that trouble is over with now, and we are not worrying about what is ahead of us.

It was thought best to make a short drive today, to merely pull up and start to enable us to go back for anything needed or forgotten. Tonight we are camped on the open prairie near Mr. Fullers and two miles from **Centropolis** —quite a name for a few pegs driven in the ground for that is all it amounts to except the hope the owner may have in it someday being a town. We trust it may not be a vain hope, but it looks that way now.

Our party consists of three families, and young men as helpers. Already our places have been assigned, that is, the order in which we are to travel. Uncle Sam Mcwhinney is the Captain of the train, he having crossed the plains in '49, has experience, of which we are so much in need, and will most likely get. His **spring wagon**, drawn by old Suze and Arch (farm horses), is to be in the lead, and Aunt Sis is to be the driver when he is elsewhere. Following this are his two baggage wagons to be looked after by some of the boys of which there are John and Hugh, his 18 and 19 year old sons, and George Haven, Enos St. John and John Newcomb, the last

named to act as helpers. The next in order is our wagon with A. O. Carpenter (my husband), myself and Henry Wilson, a 17 year old boy who, by the way, was sold to us by his father the **consideration** being that Henry receive six months schooling and that he, Mr. Wilson, receive $25.00. The boy was so hard working at home that he feels he has made quite an escape. Carlo, the white bull dog, completes our household.

The last in line is father's wagon. There is father (Thomas McCowen), mother, 16 year old sister Emily, 9 year old brother Hale, and three months old baby sister and father's man, John Fossett. To all the wagons except the one in the lead there are from two to three yoke of cattle. Cousin

"The California Pioneers" was the first song published in the newly settled territory of California.

1862

1857 **The Carpenters begin their journey to California.**

1862 **The Homestead Act promises free land to settlers in the West.**

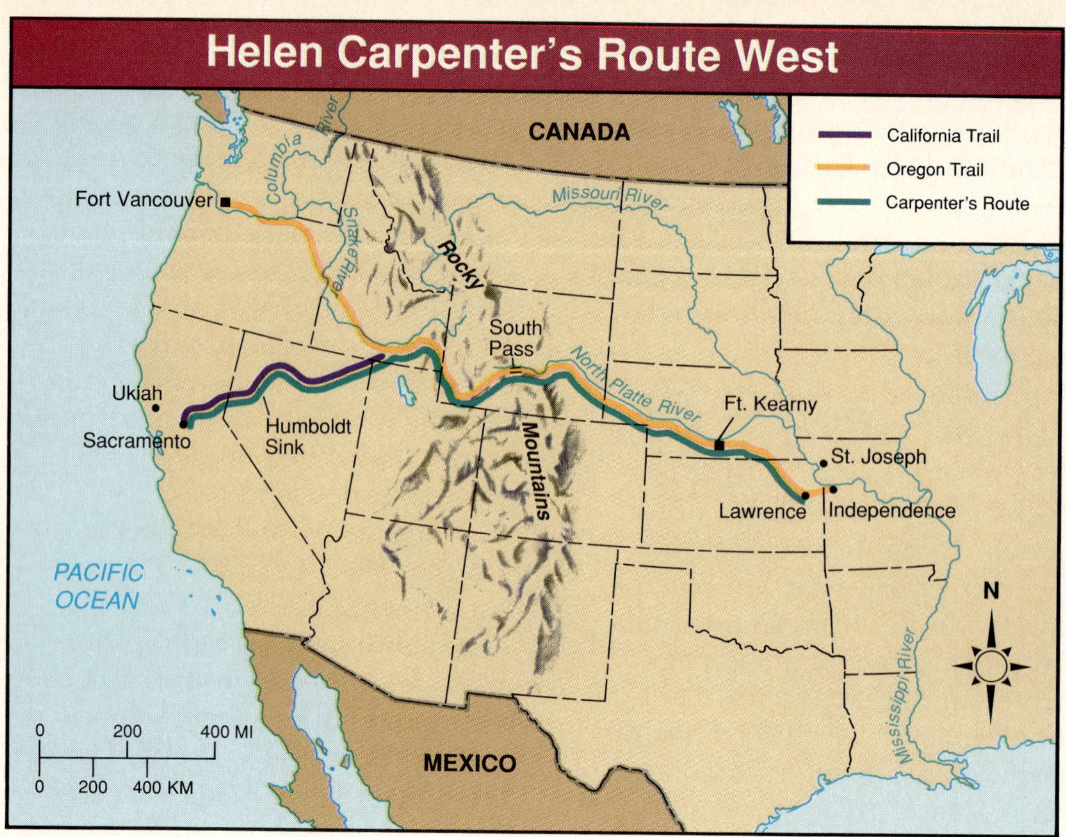

Indian pony: small wild horse trained by Native Americans

drilling: heavy fabric used to make the roof of a wagon

emigrants: people who leave one place to settle in another

bows: arches

odds and ends: different types of small articles

stowed away: stored

new fangled: new kind of

check: control

lockchains: heavy chains wrapped around a wagon's rear wheels and used to dig into the earth as the wagon was eased downhill

Dutch oven: heavy metal pot with a domelike lid

Teresa is going to ride her **Indian pony** and help the boys drive the cattle which bring up the rear of the procession. . . . When she is tired of this, she will ride in the spring wagon with her mother.

The camp tonight looks very pretty. The five wagons with white **drilling** covers (double thickness over the top) are looking very much dressed up as they stand in a semicircle in the waving green grass. . . . I am glad to have enough already cooked, for things do seem so inconvenient. Everything wanted is at the bottom. Yet our wagon gives promise of more comfort than any of the others. That, I suppose, is as it should be, for a bride should have more detail to her outfit than an ordinary **emigrants**, and although I have been married four months, this will be my bridal trip.

Our wagon has square **bows**, which makes it much more roomy than the rounded bows. Inside the cover on each side are pockets in which **odds and ends** may be **stowed away**. Then there is an "upper deck," or double floor, the supplies being packed between floors and the bed on the upper one. Henry is to sleep on the ground under the wagon. A spring seat painted bright red sits bolt upright in the front and refuses to bend or budge, regardless of size or weight, so we are not relying on this for much in the way of comfort. The greatest convenience of all, and one which none of the rest have, is a **new fangled** brake to **check** the speed in going down hill. The others have **lockchains** which are a great inconvenience and take up much time to fix and undo. All have boxes at the back of the wagons for carrying the cooking utensils. In ours there is a **Dutch oven**, a camp kettle, frying pan, and coffee pot. These, with some tin plates, tin cups, tin spoons, knives and forks, a rolling-pin, bread pan, milk can and a smoothing iron, **constitute** my entire kitchen furniture. What we are to have to eat is going to be of much more importance than how it is cooked or served. . . .

This is certainly the most beautiful country. The grass is from one to 10 feet high, and there is a **profusion** of wild flowers all over the prairie. But the violent thunderstorms are enough to wreck the nerves of **Hercules** and the rattlesnakes are as thick as the leaves on the trees, and lastly "but not leastly," the fever and **ague** are **corded up** ever ready for use. *Notwithstanding* all these *allurements*, in consideration of what we have undergone, physically and mentally, I can bid Kansas Good Bye without a regret. Still we are sorry to part with Aunt Catherine, Uncle Tom and the children. The picture they made in the old farm wagon this morning when they came to see us off will never be forgotten. Aunt Catherine looked very sad when saying she was sorry that Kansas was not good enough for us.

It was well that we came no farther today. Uncle has sent one of the boys back for something that was forgotten. We are told that it is 15 miles from here to the next **timber**.

Some pioneer families were willing to risk traveling to the West alone. Those who survived built homes on farms and ranches and set up new communities.

Crossing the plains was a long, hard, and sometimes dangerous task. Travelers often had to deal with accidents, sickness, violent weather, loss of supplies, and attacks. The Carpenters traveled about 20 miles a day. They completed their journey from Kansas to California in five months. In California they moved around and finally settled in Ukiah in 1865. Helen taught school and wrote magazine articles. She died in 1917.

From Sandra L. Myres, *Ho for California!* (San Marino, Calif., 1980), pp. 93–95. Reprinted by permission of the Henry E. Huntington Library.

Slaves' New Year's Day

❝ On one of these sale days, I saw a mother lead seven children to the auction block. **❞**

Harriet Jacobs

In 1860 nearly half the people in the South were slaves. Many were sold to landowners and worked long hours in the fields.

In the 1800s slaves were often sold at auctions. In many cases parents and their children were sold to different owners. Slaves who refused to go with their new owners were often beaten and put in jail. In this account Harriet Jacobs, who was born a slave, describes an auction day. ∾

Hiring-day at the south takes place on the 1st of January. On the 2d, the slaves are expected to go to their new masters. . . . Then comes New Year's eve; and they gather together their little alls, or . . . their little nothings, and wait anxiously for the dawning of day. At the appointed hour the grounds are **thronged** with men, women, and children, waiting, like criminals, to hear their doom pronounced. The slave is sure to know who is the most **humane**, or cruel master, within forty miles of him.

It is easy to find out, on that day, who clothes and feeds his slaves well; for he is surrounded by a crowd, begging, ''Please, massa, hire me this year. I will work *very* hard, massa.''

If a slave is unwilling to go with his new master, he is whipped, or locked up in jail, until he **consents** to go, and promises not to run away during the year. Should he chance to change his mind, thinking it justifiable to violate an **extorted** promise, woe unto him if he is caught! The whip is used till the blood flows at his feet; and his stiffened limbs are put in chains, to be dragged in the field for days and days!

thronged: crowded

humane: kind

consents: agrees

extorted: gotten by using threats

1619

1619 The first African slaves in North America arrive at the English colony of Virginia.

1808 The U.S. Congress outlaws the importation of African slaves into the United States.

If he lives until the next year, perhaps the same man will hire him again, without even giving him an opportunity of going to the hiring-ground. After those for hire are disposed of, those for sale are called up.

O, you happy free women, contrast *your* New Year's day with that of the poor **bond-woman**! With you it is a pleasant season,

Slaves were bought and sold at auctions by white owners. Young, healthy men often brought the highest prices because they were able to work the hardest.

and the light of the day is blessed. Friendly wishes meet you every where, and gifts are showered upon you. . . . Children bring their little offerings, and raise their rosy lips for a caress. They are your own, and no hand but that of death can take them from you.

But to the slave mother New Year's day comes **laden** with peculiar sorrows. She sits on her cold cabin floor, watching the children who may all be torn from her the next morning; and often does she wish that she and they might die before the day dawns. She may be an ignorant creature, **degraded** by the system that has **brutalized** her from childhood; but she has a mother's instincts, and is capable of feeling a mother's agonies.

On one of these sale days, I saw a mother lead seven children to the auction-block. She knew that *some* of them would be taken from her; but they took *all.* . . . I met that mother in the street, and her wild, **haggard** face lives to-day in my mind. . . . I had no words wherewith to comfort her.

bond-woman: female slave

laden: loaded

degraded: made to lose self-respect

brutalized: treated cruelly and violently

haggard: having a wild but tired look from grief or illness

Harriet Jacobs worked as a house servant for a doctor and his family in the mid 1800s. The doctor was cruel to his slaves. He whipped them often. Harriet fled and hid in her grandmother's tiny attic for seven years. She finally escaped to Philadelphia, where she gained her freedom. She published her autobiography in 1861.

From *Incidents in the Life of a Slave Girl*, pp. 25–27, by Harriet Jacobs, edited by Valerie Smith. The Schomburg Library of Nineteenth–Century Black Women Writers. Copyright ©1988 by Oxford University Press, Inc. Reprinted by permission.

1833 The antislavery movement grows in the northern United States.

1861

1861 The Civil War begins.

THE NATION DIVIDED

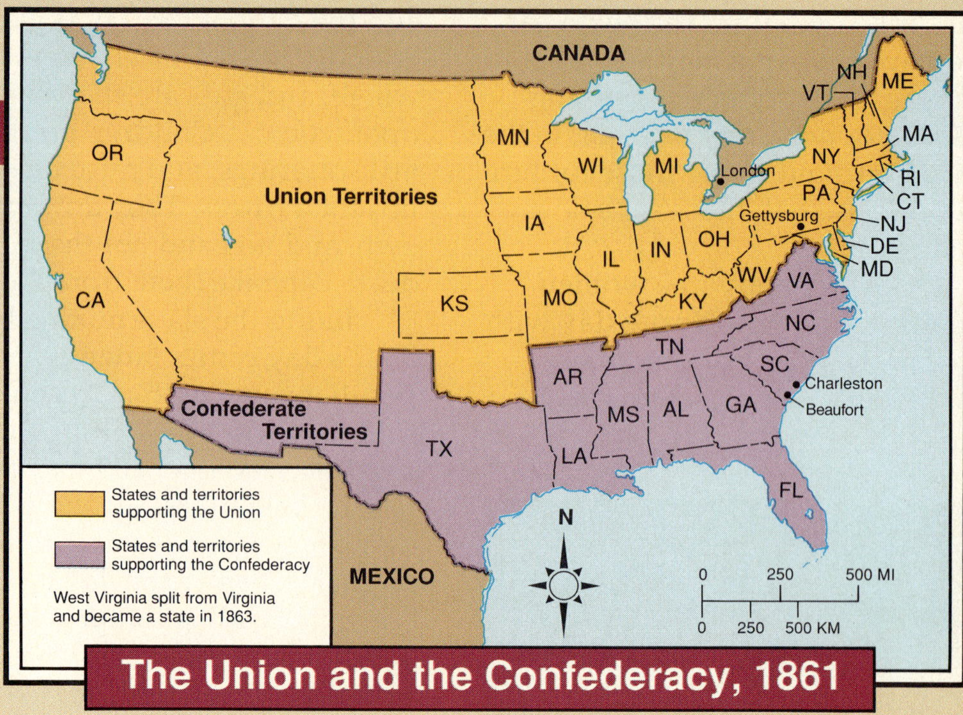

The Union and the Confederacy, 1861

seceded: pulled out of, or withdrew from, an organization

"**A** house divided against itself cannot stand." Abraham Lincoln spoke these words in 1858. The "house" was a nation not even 100 years old. It was divided between north and south. Within three years Lincoln's fears came true. By April of 1861 the southern states, 11 in all, had **seceded** from the Union. They had formed their own government. Our nation was at war.

As the new president of the United States, Lincoln did not want war. But he believed that the South had no right to form its own government.

The causes of the Civil War are complicated. Many historians believe that economic differences between the North and South were a major cause of the war. The South, with its rich soil and warm climate, had an agricultural economy. This way of life depended on the work of large numbers of slaves. In the North the soil was rocky, and the climate was cooler. The economy was based on manufacturing. Manufacturing did not rely on slaves as workers. Also, many Northerners were against slavery because they thought it was morally wrong. These **abolitionists** wanted to do away with slavery everywhere.

abolitionists: people who wanted to abolish, or do away with, slavery

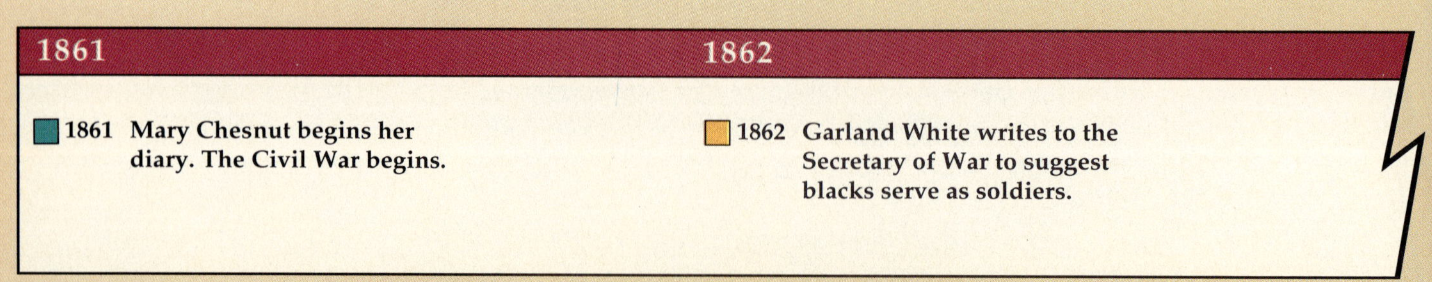

1861

1862

■ **1861** Mary Chesnut begins her diary. The Civil War begins.

■ **1862** Garland White writes to the Secretary of War to suggest blacks serve as soldiers.

At first only six southern states seceded. They formed an army and in 1861 began to take over United States forts in the South. At Fort Sumter in Charleston, South Carolina, the United States forces refused to give up the fort. The Confederates attacked, and the Civil War had begun.

The war was terrible. The battles were bloody. Families fought on different sides. And more American lives were lost than in any other war in United States history. Both at home and on the battlefield, the war changed people's lives forever.

Both sides took prisoners during the Civil War. In this painting by Winslow Homer a Union commander forces Confederate prisoners to lay down their arms.

This unit shows the effect of the Civil War on men and women from three parts of society.

- In her diary **Mary Boykin Chesnut** writes about the war from the point of view of a woman on a southern plantation.
- Letters from two black men, **Garland White** and **George Freeman**, show the desire of blacks to fight for freedom and fair treatment as soldiers.
- A letter from Union soldier **John Townsend Ketcham** to his mother describes the death of his brother in battle. A letter from Confederate soldier **Henry Owen** to his wife tells of kindness in the midst of war.

1863	1864	1865

1863 Confederate troops are defeated at the Battle of Gettysburg. Ketcham and Owen write letters home.

1865 The Civil War ends. George Freeman writes to ask for promised pay.

The War Comes Home

Mary Boykin Chesnut

Mary Boykin Chesnut was a wealthy landowner in South Carolina when the Civil War began.

Mary Boykin Chesnut and her husband James were plantation owners in South Carolina. This excerpt from Mary's diary begins as the Civil War is about to start. James and other delegates of the seceding states have chosen Jefferson Davis as president of the Confederate States. Now Confederate forces plan to attack Fort Sumter, near Charleston.

aide-de-camp: military assistant

General Beauregard: Confederate general who won the battle at Fort Sumter

adjourned: ended

telling: forceful

they: Confederate forces

blockade: Union attempt to keep European supplies from reaching Southern ports

portfolio: a case for carrying papers

April 7, 1861
Things are happening so fast.

My husband has been made an **aide-de-camp** of **General Beauregard**.

Three hours ago we were quietly packing to go home. The convention had **adjourned**.

Now he tells me the attack upon Fort Sumter may begin tonight. . . .

July 16, 1861
Now every day we grow weaker and they stronger, so we had better give a **telling** blow at once.

Already **they** begin to cry out for more ammunition, and already the **blockade** is beginning to shut it all out. . . .

I did not know there was such a "bitter cry" left in me. But I wept my heart away today when my husband went off. Things do look so black.

July 24, 1861
They brought me a Yankee soldier's **portfolio** from the battle-field. . . . One might shed a few tears over some of his letters.

1860 South Carolina becomes the first state to secede from the Union.

1861 Mary Chesnut begins her diary. The Civil War begins at Fort Sumter.

Residents of Charleston, South Carolina, watched from their rooftops as Confederate General Beauregard bombed Fort Sumter.

Women—wives and mothers—are the same everywhere. . . .

June 9, 1862
When we read of the battles in India, in Italy, in the **Crimea**—what did we care? Only an interesting topic like any other to look for in the paper.

Now you hear of a battle with a thrill and a shudder. It has come home to us. Half the people that we know in the world are under the enemy's guns.

A telegram comes to you. And you leave it on your lap. You are pale with fright. You handle it, or dread to touch it. . . . How many, many, this scrap of paper may tell you, have gone to their death.

When you meet people, sad and sorrowful is the greeting; they press your hand, tears stand in their eyes or roll down their cheeks, as they happen to have more or less self-control. They have brothers, fathers, or sons—as the case may be—in the battle. And this thing now seems never to stop. We have no breathing time given us. It cannot be so at the North, for the papers say gentlemen do not go in the ranks there. They are officers or clerks of departments, **&c&c&c**. Then, we see so many foreign regiments among our prisoners. Germans—Irish—Scotch. The proportion of trouble is awfully against us. Every company on the field is filled with our nearest and dearest—**rank and file**, common soldiers.

Miriam's story today:

A woman she knew heard her son was killed—had hardly taken in the horror of it, when they came to say it was all a mistake—mistake of name. She fell on her knees with a shout of joy. . . . The household were totally upset. The swing back of the **pendulum** from the scene of weeping and wailing of a few moments before was very exciting. In the midst of this hubbub, the **hearse** drove up with the poor boy in his metallic coffin.

Does anybody wonder so many women die? Grief and constant anxiety kill nearly as many women as men die on the battlefield. Miriam's friend is at the point of death with brain fever; the sudden changes from

Crimea: a region in southern Russia; the site of a war in 1853 between Russia and Turkey

&c&c&c: (et cetera) and so on

rank and file: the enlisted common soldier

pendulum: something that goes back and forth between two extremes

hearse: a wagon for carrying the dead

1865

1863 Union forces win at Gettysburg and Vicksburg.

1864 General Sherman marches from Chattanooga, Tennessee, to Savannah, Georgia.

1865 Lee surrenders to Grant at Appomattox. Mary Chesnut's diary ends.

Confederate soldiers were prepared for
fighting. Many grew up in the country and
learned to use guns at an early age.

joy to grief were more than she
could bear.

January 31, 1864
Today for a pair of **forlorn** shoes,
I gave 85 dollars. . . . Mr. Pettigrew
says you take your money to
market in the market basket and
bring home what you buy in your
pocketbook.

May 27, 1864
I was telling them today of a
woman who came to **Mrs. Davis**
in **Richmond**, hoping to get her
help. She wanted her husband's
pardon. She was shabbily dressed,
chalk white and pinched in her
face. . . . She was strong, and her
way of telling her story was hard
and cold enough. She told it sim-
ply, but over and over again. . . .
     The army had to pass so near
her. Poor little Susie had just died,
and the boy was **ailing**. Food was
so scarce and so bad. They all had
chills. She was so miserable. The
negroes had all gone to the Yan-
kees. There was nobody to cut

wood, and it was so cold. They
were coming so near. "I wrote—
and I wrote—if **you** want to see
the baby alive, come. If they won't
let you—come anyhow. *You see, I
did it*—if he is a **deserter**.
     "He said they would not let
him come. Only colonels and
generals can get **furloughs** now.
He only intended to stay one day,
but we **coaxed** and begged him,
and then he stayed and stayed,
and he was afraid afterward to go
back. He did not mean to be a
coward nor to desert. So he went
on the gunboats on the river, to
serve there. And then some of his
old officers saw him. And they
would not believe his story. . . .
They are going to shoot him. I
would not let him alone. You see,
I did it. *Don't you see?*"
     Mrs. Davis was gone ever so
long. And the stiff, cold woman,
white as wall, sat there and told it
to me many times. I wanted to go
home, but she clutched me. . . .
     Mrs. Davis came in, smiling.
     "Here **it** is—all that you want."
     The creature stood straight
up—then fell down on the sofa
pillow, sobbing as if soul and
body would come **asunder**. So I
fled—rather blind myself. . . .

June 2, 1864
Gone today for 2 lbs. of tea, 40 lbs.
of coffee, and 60 lbs. of sugar—
800 dollars. . . .

February 16, 1865
Lincolnton, North Carolina
     My ideas of those last days
are confused.
     The Martins left Columbia the
Friday before I did. . . .
     Then I met Mr. Christopher
Hampton. . . . He said it was time to
move on, **Sherman** at Orangeburg
was barely a day's journey from

Columbia, and that he left a track as bare and blackened as a fire in the prairies.

So my time had come, too. My husband urged me to go home. He said Camden would be safe enough. They had no **spite** to that old town—as they have to Charleston and Columbia. Molly, weeping and wailing, came in while we were at table, wiping her red-hot face with her cook's grimy apron. She said I ought to go among our own black people on the plantation. They would take care of me better than anyone else. So I agreed to go to Mulberry or the Hermitage plantation. . . .

April 7, 1865
Richmond has fallen—and I have no heart to write about it. **Grant** broke through our lines. Sherman cut through them. . . .

They are too many for us.
Everything lost in Richmond, even our **archives**.
Blue-black is our horizon.

June 4, 1865
Went up to my old house, "Kamchatka." The Trapiers live there now. . . . I do not think I ever did as much weeping—or as bitter—in the same space of time. I let myself go. It did me good. I cried with a will.

He prayed that we might have strength to stand up and bear our bitter disappointment, to look on our ruined homes and our desolated country and be strong.

spite: hate, bad feelings

Grant: Union General Ulysses S. Grant

archives: old public papers or historical records; also, the place where such papers are kept

He: Mr. Trapier

This painting shows General Sherman on his march through Georgia. Union armies destroyed railroads, stole crops, and burned cities.

When the war ended, Mary and James Chesnut went to live on his father's plantation. The buildings and land were damaged, and all of the cotton had been burned. Most of the family's possessions had been stolen. The Chesnuts found enough food in their garden to live on. Mary Chesnut continued to write in her diary until July, but her entries were full of sadness. The way of life she had known was gone forever.

Reprinted from *Mary Chesnut's Civil War*, ed. C. Vann Woodward (New Haven, Conn.: Yale University Press, 1981), pp. 101, 108, 313, 370–71, 552, 610, 611, 613, 715, 824. Reprinted by permission of the publisher. Copyright © 1981 by Yale University Press.

Fighting to Be Free

" . . . slavery . . . is the cause of all our trouble."

Garland H. White

Of the 180,000 black soldiers who fought for the Union during the Civil War, more than 120,000 were slaves who had fled the South.

The Northern forces began to hire black troops in 1863. As the first letter shows, many blacks were eager to fight to end slavery. But even as soldiers, as the second letter shows, blacks were often treated unfairly. The letters have many spelling and punctuation errors. In many states it was illegal for blacks to be taught to read and write.

sir: the secretary of war, Edwin M. Stanton

indulg: (indulge) allow

tender: offer

Hon: your Honor; polite form of addressing Stanton

speculation: self-gain

restoration: return

London Canada West May 7th 1862

dear **sir**. please **indulg** me the liberty of writing you afew lines upon a subject of grave importance to your & my country. . . . My name is G. H. White formerly the Servant of Robert Toombs of Georgia. . . . I am now a minister, & am called upon By my peopel to **tender** to your *Hon* thir willingness to serve as soldiers in the southern parts during the summer season or longer if required. our offer is not for **speculation** or self interest but for our love for the north & the government at large, & at the same time we pray god that the triumph of the north & **restoration** of peace if I may call it will prove an eternal overthrow of the institution of slavery which is the cause of all our trouble   if you desire to see me let me

1862

1862 Garland White writes to the secretary of war to suggest blacks serve as soldiers.

1863 After the Emancipation Proclamation many former slaves join the Northern army.

hear at an early day. I am certain of raising a good **no.** in the west
& in the north. . . . please let me hear from your Hon soon   your
most humble servant

Garland H. White

please excuse my bad writing as I never went to School a day in
my **left**. I learnd what little I know by the hardest. . . .

no.: number

left: (life)

General Hospitle Beaufort SC
June 25th 1865.

Dear, **Sir**, I am under the painfull necesity of writing you a few
lines for **Redresse**   I hav been in The Sirvice of the united states
since Nov fifth one thousand eight hundred and sixty four and hav
never recieve pay but twice once in June sixty four and then in,
August   What you paid me in June was seven **doll**. Per months
I hav not recieved my Back pay From the government yet   I am a
man of faimley a Wife and two small children   I was foold in the
first place   my famley Recieves no Relief from my state as was
Promesed me. . . . as you are one of the head of our great governent
I write you for assistance   I want them to Give me my discharge
and let me go and worke and suporte my Familey for they are
nearly starved and hav not suitabal cloathing. . . . my familey de-
pends upon my daily labor for their suporte. . . . now the ware is
over I think that it is no moore than wright that I should Have my
Discharge. . . . If I hav don wrong in writing to my superior i pray
Pardon me For so doing   But I should like to Recieve some money
from the governent and go and see after my fanliey   Nomore From
your moste humble Servent and Solgier

George G Freeman

Sir: the chief justice
of the United States,
Salmon P. Chase

Redresse: (redress)
a solution or relief

doll: (dollars)

By the end of the war one in eight soldiers was black. Of the 180,000
blacks who served in the Union army during the Civil War, about 35,000
lost their lives fighting. Twenty-three were awarded the Medal of Honor.
This was the highest award for heroism in battle.

From _Freedom: A Documentary History of Emancipation 1861–1867_, ed. Ira Berlin, Joseph
Reidy, and Leslie Rowland (New York: Cambridge University Press, 1982), pp. 82, 379.
Reprinted by permission of the publisher.

**1864   Congress grants black
soldiers equal pay.**

**1865   The Civil War ends.
George Freeman writes
to ask for promised pay.**

From the Battlefield

❝ I told him . . . unless they stopped the war we would fight them for a thousand years. . . . ❞

Captain Henry Owen

The Battle of Gettysburg began as a chance skirmish between Union and Confederate troops. Casualties totaled more than 40,000.

The effect of the Civil War is best seen in the stories of people from the North and South. The first letter below was written by Union soldier John Townsend Ketcham to his mother. He describes his brother's death in the Battle of Gettysburg, July 1–3, 1863. In the second letter Confederate Captain Henry Owen describes a morning he spent with a captured Union officer. ➳

Frederick City: a small town just south of Gettysburg

thee: you

regiment: large group of soldiers. Edward and John were in Company M, 4th New York Cavalry.

batteries: guns and cannon

sharpshooter's: belonging to a person who shoots a gun well

temple: the side of the forehead

Frederick City
July 8th, 1863

Dear Mother:

I telegraphed to **thee** as soon as I could, and wrote about Edward. I cannot realize that he is dead. Don't let it kill thee, mother! Thee and I are all that is left of us.

Edward was the first man killed in the **regiment**. They were lying on the ground, behind a little mill, in front of our **batteries**, making a part of the outer line of battle. It is always necessary in such time for someone to keep a lookout to watch the movements of the enemy. As the men all lay on their faces, Edward was sitting up to look; a **sharpshooter's** bullet probably struck him in the **temple**, and went through his head. He put up his hand, and said: "Oh!" and fell on his elbow, quite dead. . . .

Apr. 1861		
Apr. 1861 The Civil War begins.	**Apr. 1862 The South drafts soldiers.**	**Mar. 1863 The North passes a draft law.**

Pretty soon the rebels came out from their works, in heavy
force, and advanced in line. Our batteries **commenced** to mow
them down, and the men lay down until in close range; then the
outer line raised up, and the two lines fought, without either mov-
ing from their place. It was a grand, but terrible sight! The rebels
concentrated on one part of our line, and pressed it back, to charge
our **breastworks**; our **flanks** closed in on them, and hundreds were
driven in, prisoners, while the rest ran back to their lines like
sheep. One poor fellow came in just by me; the first words he said
were, ''Gentlemen, I do this because I am forced to.''

I went out at night, to look for Edward, but could not find
him. The next morning our line advanced, and I went out to the
tree; and there, on his back, his hands peacefully on his breast,
lay all that was left of the brother I have lived so closely with
all my life. His features, though discolored and swollen, had an
expression I have seen on them before—peaceful rest. He had lain
thirty-six hours on the field, with the roaring of cannon and burst-
ing of shells over him, and the feet of **contending hosts**, of dark-
ness and freedom, trampling the ground he lay on.

When I got him, I brought him down under a tree. A Captain
of one of the batteries said to me, ''If he were a brother of mine, I
would bury him on the field of glory.'' He was very kind, and sent
me men to dig the grave. In a little grove behind the batteries,
under an oak tree, in his soldier's uniform, wrapped in a shelter-
tent, lies all the earthly remains of my brother. ''He has gone to be
a soldier in the army of the Lord.'' And mother, thee and I walk
this world of sorrow. . . .

Edward has marched many a weary mile; he has lain on the
wet, cold ground, with nothing over him, long nights, with the rain
pouring on him, and never murmured; he has lain and shivered in
the snow and slush, all long winter nights, after weary marches,
hungry, perhaps, or after eating a few hard crackers, and a little
raw meat; and, in his discomfort, he has never wished for home;
except, perhaps, to look forward to that bright day when the rebel-
lion would be crushed, and he should return home, war-worn, and
covered with his well worn honors. That day, alas! he can never
see. Oh God! Thy price for freedom is a *dear one!*

John

commenced: began

breastworks: walls built quickly for defense, about chest high

flanks: troops positioned along the sides

contending hosts: fighting armies

<table>
<tr><td></td><td>May 1865</td></tr>
<tr><td>July 1863 Confederate troops are
defeated at the Battle of
Gettysburg. Ketcham and
Owen write letters.</td><td>May 1865 The last Confederate troops
surrender. The Civil War
ends.</td></tr>
</table>

Bunker Hill
Berkely Co., Va.
July 18th, 1863

My Dear Harriet:

After the great battle of Gettysburg, our **division** had charge of a large **lot** of prisoners, some two hundred officers and thirty-three hundred privates. We guarded them from Gettysburg to Winchester, and had charge of them eight days. Our **provisions** were scarce. . . .

One day while at Williamsport, on this side of the Potomac, I went along the line of **sentinels** to see if all was safe. As I went strolling by a crowd, I found a young, fine looking officer trying to trade off a neat little pocket **flask**, silver mounted, for a **half cake** of bread. Our soldiers were trying to see how small a piece he would agree to take. I told this officer that he would soon have beef and flour issued to him and advised him to wait awhile, but he said he had never cooked any and did not know how to fix up his flour and beef. He said he was very hungry and wanted a piece of bread.

Some officers standing by were trying to **dispute** with him about the war, but he told them that he was a prisoner and it was unfair to ask him to argue the matter since if he spoke his **sentiments** freely they would be offended and that any arguments they might have would not affect the war at all nor end the **strife** a day sooner. They **persisted**, but he kept his eye and mind fixed upon the bread. I tried to get him off from the **party**. I had not gotten my **rations** that day and it was nine o'clock. I told him, however, that as soon as they came I would divide with him.

Soon afterwards, one of my men told me that he knew a house not far off where I could get breakfast. I went and got the yankee officer and told him if he would promise not to try to escape I would take him out to breakfast. He readily promised, and away we went over hill and dale together without even a pistol, chattering gaily as we **promenaded** together. We reached the house and got a splendid breakfast. The old lady and their daughters saw my old gray uniform and the yankee's dark blue cloth and they stirred about like the house was on fire. We were both very hungry and ate heartily of the old lady's light bread, fried ham, coffee (**genuine**) and honey.

When we got through, the old lady did not want to take my Confederate money. The yankee pulled out a full purse of his **green backs** and paid her for both of us. He then purchased three dozen biscuits and we jogged along back to camp. He was very thankful for my kindness and wanted me to accept his flask as a present, but I told him I did not charge for favors and that I had only done my duty to my fellow man in **distress**. He said I had fulfilled the **scriptures**, in that when I found mine enemy **a-hungered** I fed him. I told him that was my religion.

His flask was the neatest one I ever saw—silver mounted and covered with bamboo and whalebone, with a nice cord. It was all he had to carry water in, and I did not think it right to accept it. I told him all I wanted of his people was to be let alone, and unless they stopped the war we would fight them for a thousand years. . . .

Yours faithfully as ever,
Henry

The Civil War was the first American war to be photographed. This photo taken by Matthew Brady shows a wounded Union soldier after his capture by the Confederate army.

Mrs. Ketcham experienced a second loss before the war ended. Her son John was captured by Confederate troops not long after he wrote his letter home. He died in a Confederate prisoner-of-war camp on October 8, 1863. Nothing is known about the fate of Henry Owen.

From *The Brothers' War*, ed. Annette Tapert (New York: Times Books, 1988), pp. 149–152, 163–165. Letter written by Henry T. Owen is from the Personal Papers Collection (Accession 28154), Archives and Records Division, Virginia State Library and Archives, Richmond, Virginia.

THE NEW FRONTIER

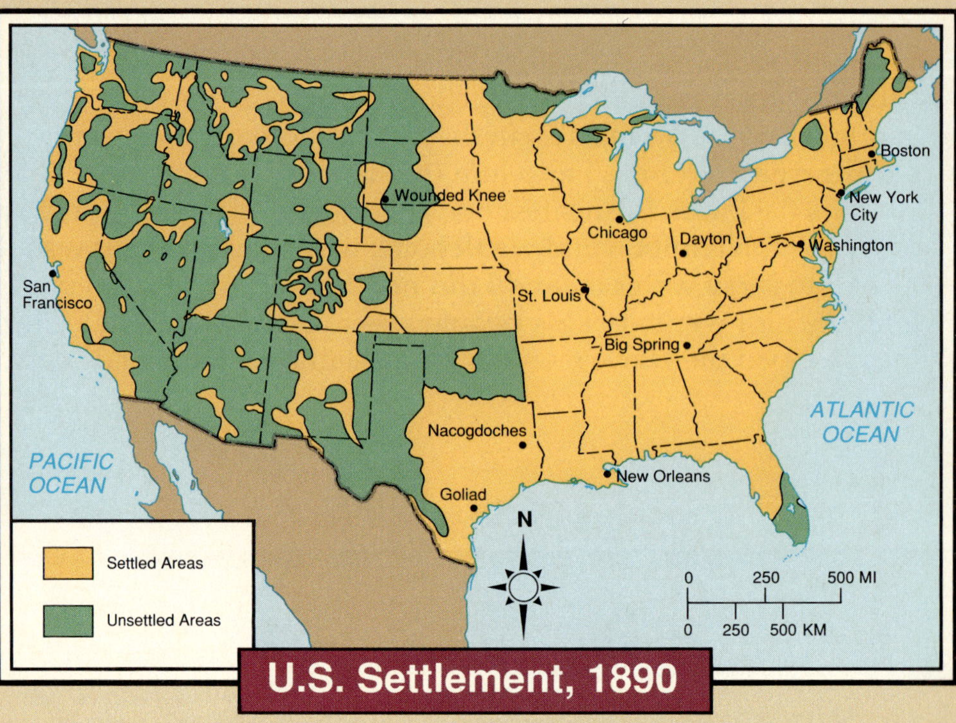

U.S. Settlement, 1890

prejudiced: disliking or not trusting someone because of race, religion, sex, or nationality

Great Plains: the wide, level stretch of land east of the Rocky Mountains

range: unfenced land on which cattle roam and graze

When the Civil War ended in 1865, Americans in the South faced many problems. Cities, roads, fields, and factories were in ruins. Four million former slaves needed homes and jobs. And southern states needed to find ways to protect the rights of black Americans.

Reconstruction, the process of bringing the South back into the Union, lasted from 1865 to 1877. During this time Congress passed laws to protect the rights of black people. But many Southerners were still **prejudiced** against blacks. Many white Southerners tried to keep blacks from voting and getting good jobs. For many former slaves life was not much better than it had been before the war.

Many Southerners, both black and white, headed west to the **Great Plains.** There they hoped to find better jobs and a better life. At first there was plenty of land for all. Settlers simply claimed a piece of land to farm. Ranchers let their cattle roam across the broad **range**. Many people found work on farms or ranches.

For the Native Americans of the Great Plains, this westward movement was a disaster. The new settlers pushed them off their

1865	1870	1875

1865 The Civil War ends. Congress sets up the Freedmen's Bureau to aid freed slaves.

1875 Cattle ranches have spread across the Great Plains from Texas to Montana.

tribal homelands. White hunters killed the buffalo they needed for survival.

By 1890 the buffalo herds were almost gone. Farms and ranches had taken the place of ancient hunting grounds. The Great Plains tribes were angry about losing their lands. Fighting broke out between them and the settlers. The government sent soldiers to fight the Native Americans. Some tribes were forced to live on **reservations**.

Meanwhile, more and more land was fenced off for farming. There was not enough room for new ranches or settlers. So people kept moving westward. By 1912 all of the land from coast to coast had been carved into states. The western frontier was gone.

The large buffalo herds that once roamed the Great Plains were important to the Native Americans. By 1890 the great herds were almost gone.

This unit describes some of the changes Americans faced as the nation recovered from the war and spread westward.

- In a letter to his old master, **Jourdon Anderson** compares his life as a slave to his life as a free man.
- In an interview **Elario Cardova** describes his life as a cowboy in the late 1800s.
- **Black Elk** tells how white soldiers overwhelmed the Sioux at Wounded Knee, South Dakota.

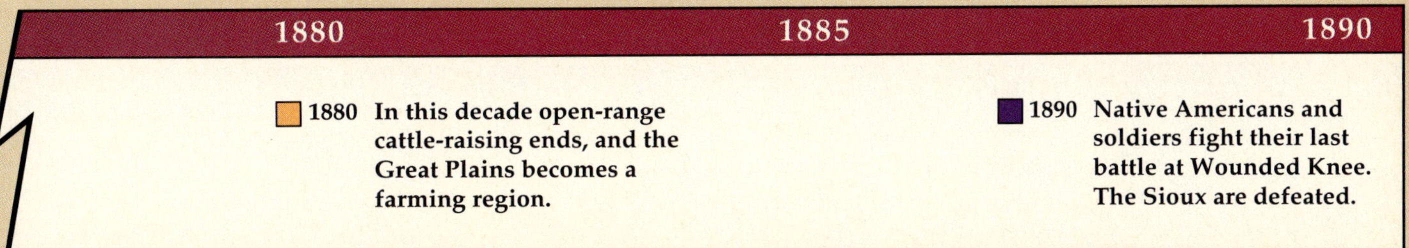

Free at Last

> **❝** Here I draw my wages every Saturday night; but in Tennessee there was never any pay-day for the Negroes any more than for the horses and cows. **❞**
>
> **Jourdon Anderson**

This painting, *On to Liberty* by Theodor Kaufmann, shows slaves crossing Union lines in search of freedom.

Jourdon Anderson, a slave, escaped to freedom in the North during the Civil War. Thousands more slaves had to wait for the South's defeat before they tasted freedom. For these new citizens hopes ran high after the war. Anderson wrote the following letter to his former master, Colonel Anderson. The plantation owner had asked Jourdon to return "home" after the war.

harboring Rebs: giving shelter to Confederate soldiers, sometimes called Rebels

To my old Master, Colonel P. H. Anderson, Big Spring, Tennessee.

Sir. I got your letter, and was glad to find that you had not forgotten Jourdon, and that you wanted me to come back and live with you again, promising to do better for me than anybody else can. I have often felt uneasy about you. I thought the Yankees would have hung you long before this, for **harboring Rebs** they found at your house. . . . Although you shot at me twice before I left you, I did not want to hear of your being hurt, and am glad you are still living. . . .

Now if you will write and say what wages you will give me, I will be better able to decide whether it would be to my advantage to move back again. As to my freedom, which you say I can have,

1865		
1865 Congress sets up the Freedmen's Bureau to aid freed slaves. Some Southern states restrict blacks' rights.	**1867** The Reconstruction Acts put the South under military rule until states grant basic rights to blacks.	**1868** The Fourteenth Amendment makes all blacks full U.S. citizens.

there is nothing to be gained on that score, as I got my **free papers**
in 1864. . . . Mandy says she would be afraid to go back without
some proof that you were **disposed** to treat us justly and kindly; and
we have **concluded** to test your **sincerity** by asking you to send us
our wages for the time we served you. This will make us forget
and forgive old scores, and rely on your justice and friendship in
the future. I served you faithfully for thirty-two years, and Mandy
twenty years. At twenty-five dollars a month for me, and two
dollars a week for Mandy, our earnings would amount to eleven
thousand six hundred and eighty dollars. Add to this the **interest**
for the time our wages have been kept back, and **deduct** what you
paid for our clothing, and three doctor's visits to me, and pulling
a tooth for Mandy, and the balance will show what we are in
justice **entitled to.** Please send the money by Adam's Express, in
care of V. Winters, **Esq.**, Dayton, Ohio. If you fail to pay us for
faithful labors in the past, we can have little faith in your promises
in the future. We trust the good Maker has opened your eyes to
the wrongs which you and your fathers have done to me and
my fathers, in making us **toil** for you for generations without
recompense. Here I **draw my wages** every Saturday night; but
in Tennessee there was never any pay-day for the Negroes any
more than for the horses and cows. Surely there will be a day of
reckoning for those who **defraud** the laborer of his hire.

    In answering this letter . . . please state if there has been any
schools opened for the colored children in your neighborhood. The
great desire of my life now is to give my children an education, and
have them form **virtuous** habits.

    Say howdy to George Carter, and thank him for taking the
pistol from you when you were shooting at me.

From your old servant,
Jourdon Anderson

free papers: legal documents that stated a person was free

disposed: willing

concluded: made up our minds

sincerity: honesty

interest: extra money owed as a penalty for withholding payment

deduct: take out

entitled to: have a right to receive

Esq.: (Esquire) used as a title for a gentleman

toil: work

recompense: payment

draw my wages: receive my pay

reckoning: judging

defraud: cheat

virtuous: good

Colonel Anderson probably did not accept Jourdon's terms. We have no
record of Jourdon Anderson's life as a free man. For most former slaves,
though, life remained hard. The early years of Reconstruction improved
the lives of many blacks, but these changes did not last. The struggle of
blacks for equal rights was only beginning.

From *The Black Americans: A History in Their Own Words*, ed. Milton Meltzer
(New York: Thomas Y. Crowell, 1984), pp. 83–85.

	1877
1870 The Fifteenth Amendment guarantees black men the right to vote.	**1877** Southern states begin passing laws to segregate public places.

A Home on the Range

> " I . . . calculated I would be working on a farm unless I followed the westward movement of the ranches."

Elario Cardova

Artist Frederic Remington painted many western scenes. In this painting he shows a cowboy cutting off a cattle stampede.

Elario Cardova was born on a farm in Texas in 1861. At the age of ten he left home to work on a cattle ranch. He performed many different tasks in the 11 years he spent as a cowboy. During this time the cattle business was growing quickly. Meanwhile, more and more people were moving westward and claiming their own small piece of the range.

Nacogdoches County: a county in eastern Texas near the Louisiana border

under cultivation: used for growing crops

work stock: horses

tracts: areas

I was born on November 3, 1861, at my father's farm seven miles east of **Nacogdoches County**. So far as I know I have remained in the state the remainder of my life. Whether or not I have done wisely and have remained in the best state of these United States, I cannot say. . . .

My parents were born in the Nacogdoches section. My grandparents came to America from Spain. My grandmother's family, on my mother's side of the family, came to Texas from Barcelona, Spain, at the time Spain ruled this section of America. . . .

Our farm consisted of about fifty acres **under cultivation** and about fifty acres in pasture for our milk cows and **work stock.** In addition to our farming, we owned longhorn cattle which ranged on the unsettled land. Farms were all fenced and were situated far apart, leaving great **tracts** of land for the cattle to graze on. To tell you how many cattle we owned is impossible. The number may have been five hundred or a thousand. We didn't give the cattle any attention. The cattle bred and multiplied at their will and found their own

1862

1862 The Homestead Act offers 160 acres of western land to any head of a family willing to farm it for 5 years.

1865 At the end of the Civil War, Northerners are eager to buy Texas cattle to restock their herds.

1869 The first transcontinental railroad links West and East.

living on the range where it suited their taste. . . .

I, as all other boys of those days, learned to ride a **mustang** at an early age. I could ride a gentle **hoss** at the age of five and could handle a ordinary mustang, for all general purposes, at the age of ten years. . . .

The cattle range was about the only place a young farm boy could **secure employment. Consequently,** I went to the open-range country where large ranches were established, and I chose **Goliad County** as the place to find work. I was successful and was given work on a ranch owned by the Hughes brothers. That was in 1871. . . .

I was no **precocious** child in size or ability, but I was above the average ten-year-old boy in size. I told the folks I was twelve years old and could easily pass myself off as being that age. I, not having ever been away from home, was somewhat **verdant**, and my experience handling cattle was limited to what I had learned assisting my folks to handle our cattle.

The Hughes **outfit** ranged their cattle **adjacent** to the **San Antonio River**, and during a wet period **bog** holes became numerous. The outfit needed someone to keep a watch for **bogged** critters. The work did not require a top hand or one with the strength of a man. I could meet the requirements, and there began my career as a cowhand.

My mount did the hard part of my job, and that was pulling bogged critters out of the holes. When I located a bogged

Hired cowhands earned about $30 a month in 1870. During a cattle drive they gathered around the chuck wagon for their meals and slept under the open sky.

mustang: a type of horse

hoss: horse

secure employment: find a job

consequently: as a result

Goliad County: a county in southeastern Texas

precocious: showing advanced qualities at an early age

verdant: green; lacking experience

outfit: ranch owners and the people who work for them

adjacent: next to

San Antonio River: river that flows from San Antonio southeast to the Guadalupe River

bog: very wet and spongy

bogged: stuck or sunken

1880

1875   For the next ten years Dodge City, Kansas, is the largest cattle market in the world.

1880   In this decade open-range cattle-raising ends, and the Great Plains becomes a farming region.

animal, I put the loop around its horns, with the rope tied to the saddle horn, and the hoss then did the hauling, pulling from the saddle. . . .

I was paid fifteen dollars a month at the start of my cowboy career and at the end of two years was receiving twenty-five dollars as my monthly pay. . . .

I graduated to the regular general cowhand's work after the second year, and then I lived behind the **chuck wagon** about half of the time. The general spring and fall roundups kept us busy about six months of the year. . . .

The roundups were **participated** in by all the cattlemen of the section. The different brands would be separated and the strays driven back to their home range. The roundup crews worked from one section of the range to another, and when the roundup was completed, all the cattle would be on their home range. Then again, from time to time a few would stray off, **principally** during storms, so by the time the next roundup was

held, the various brands would be more or less mixed.

The branding of the range cattle was done during the roundup. The branding was performed by a branding crew. The **cutting crew** would call out the brand to be applied as the calf was being dragged to where the irons were being heated in a fire. The **cutters** would note the mother cow's brand and yell to the brand man. For instance, suppose they called for BH, then the brander would answer, "BH," and then the checker would repeat the letters. The BH brand would be applied and noted in the record book. At the end of the roundup, each outfit was given a record of the number of their calves branded. . . .

My career on the range was during the period when there was a great deal of conflict among the ranchers of the Goliad range territory. I happened to **secure** a job with an outfit which was not only called **rustlers**, but were classed as one of the leaders of the rustlers. However, they **maintained** that they were

Thousands of longhorn cattle were raised on the grassy plains of Texas. Cowboys drove the large thundering herds across rivers and miles of dusty trails to market.

defending the rights of the small ranchers against the **impositions** of the large ranchers. . . .

During the Civil War and for a period after the war **ceased,** branding was neglected by many cattlemen. Also, very few cattle were sent to market, because the market was cut off from Texas. The lack of sales resulted in a large increase of cattle. Therefore, the two conditions produced thousands of cattle which were unbranded.

A few years after the war ceased, railroads extended west into Kansas, and markets were established within driving distance of Texas. Then the prices went up which resulted in a scramble to brand those cattle without a brand. Naturally, ranchers maintained they had a **superior** claim to the unbranded cattle within the section which they called their home range, and any unbranded cattle grazing with the cattle carrying their brand. This claim was generally accepted as proper, but there were some folks who did not **confine** their branding **strictly** within their territory. Branding cattle in territory claimed by some other rancher led to trouble and many killings. . . .

The matter was **eventually** settled by the **Rangers** and other officials taking a hand in the matter, and the unbranded cattle finally disappeared, which removed the main cause of the **strife**. . . .

During the later part of the eleven-year period I worked for the Hughes outfit, the country began to change from open to a fenced range. . . .

I **foresaw** the **elimination** of the open range in Goliad County and calculated I would be working on a farm unless I followed the westward movement of the ranches. This situation caused me to return to Nacogdoches County and engage in farming, which I followed for a number of years. In my middle life I **discontinued** farming and entered the **mercantile** business and I have followed the business up to date.

This painting by Thomas Eakins shows one way cowboys entertained themselves. Many historic cowboy songs are still sung today.

Elario Cardova was right. The days of the open range soon came to an end. The invention of better farm machinery made it possible for farmers to grow grain on the dry Great Plains. As farmers fenced off pieces of the range, cattle ranchers pushed farther west. Railroad lines and new towns pushed the frontier back. New states were carved from the land. The open range was a thing of the past.

From Jim Lanning and Judy Lanning (eds.), *Texas Cowboys: Memories of the Early Days* (College Station: Texas A&M University Press, 1984), pp. 177–86. Reprinted by permission of the publisher.

---

impositions: unfair practices

ceased: ended

superior: first, best

confine: limit

strictly: only

eventually: at last

Rangers: Texas Rangers who kept law and order

strife: trouble

foresaw: knew beforehand

elimination: end

discontinued: quit

mercantile: trade

Tragedy at Wounded Knee

" . . . the women and children were running away and trying to hide. . . . "

Black Elk

Some Native Americans performed the Ghost Dance, a religious ceremony that they hoped would bring back their old way of life.

Sioux: a group of Native Americans living in the north central plains. They called themselves *Dakota,* meaning "allies" or "friends."

In December 1890 the U.S. military learned that the **Sioux** were holding a ceremony known as the Ghost Dance. Soldiers thought the Ghost Dance would lead to a Sioux revolt. U.S. troops took a group of Sioux to Wounded Knee Creek in South Dakota. As the soldiers took away the Sioux weapons, a shot was fired. A bloody battle followed. Soldiers killed more than 200 unarmed Sioux. Black Elk, a young Sioux, describes the tragedy.

. . . In the morning I went out after my horses, and while I was out I heard shooting off toward the east, and I knew from the sound that it must be wagon-guns (cannon) going off. The sounds went right through my body, and I felt that something terrible would happen.

When I reached camp with the horses, a man rode up to me and said: "Hey-hey-hey! The people that are coming are fired on! I know it!"

buckskin: horse

I saddled up my **buckskin** and put on my **sacred** shirt. It was

sacred: holy

one I had made to be worn by no one but myself. It had a spotted eagle outstretched on the back of it, and the daybreak star was on the left shoulder, because when facing south that shoulder is toward the east. Across the breast, from the left shoulder to the right hip, was the flaming rainbow, and there was another rainbow around the neck, like a necklace, with a star at the bottom. At each shoulder, elbow, and wrist was an eagle feather; and over the whole shirt were red streaks of lightning. You will see that this was from my

1824	
1824 **The U.S. government creates the Bureau of Indian Affairs to deal with Native Americans.**	**1830** **Congress passes the Indian Removal Act. Native Americans are moved west of the Mississippi.**

great vision, and you will know how it protected me that day.

I painted my face all red, and in my hair I put one eagle feather for the **One Above**. . . .

I started out alone on the old road that ran across the hills to Wounded Knee. I had no gun. I carried only the sacred bow of the west that I had seen in my great vision. I had gone only a little way when a band of young men came galloping after me. . . .

We rode fast, and there were about twenty of us now. The shooting was getting louder. A horseback from over there came galloping very fast toward us, and he said: "Hey-hey-hey! They have murdered them!" Then he whipped his horse and rode away faster toward Pine Ridge. . . .

We stopped on the ridge not far from the head of the dry **gulch**. Wagon guns were still going off over there on the little hill, and they were going off again where they hit along the gulch. There was much shooting down yonder, and there were many cries, and we could see cavalrymen scattered over the hills ahead of us. Cavalrymen were riding along the gulch and shooting into it, where the women and children were running away and trying to hide in the **gullies** and the **stunted** pines. . . .

We stopped back behind the ridge, and I said to the others: "Take courage. These are our relatives. We will try to get them back." Then we all sang a song which went like this:

> "A **thunder being nation**
> I am, I have said.
> A thunder being nation I am,
> I have said.
> You shall live.
> You shall live.
> You shall live.
> You shall live."

Soldiers sometimes attacked Sioux camps without warning. White soldiers armed with rifles greatly outnumbered the Sioux.

		1890
1876 The Sioux defeat U.S. forces at the Battle of Little Bighorn.	**1887** Congress passes the Dawes Act. Native American territory is broken up into small farming units.	**1890** U.S. troops kill more than 200 unarmed Sioux at Wounded Knee, marking the final defeat of the Sioux.

This type of shirt was worn by the Sioux during the Ghost Dance. They thought the shirt had special powers that would protect them from enemy bullets.

Then I rode over the ridge and the others after me, and we were crying: "Take courage! It is time to fight!" The soldiers who were guarding our relatives shot at us and then ran away fast, and some more cavalrymen on the other side of the gulch did too. We got our relatives and sent them across the ridge to the northwest where they would be safe.

I had no gun, and when we were charging, I just held the sacred bow out in front of me with my right hand. The bullets did not hit us at all. . . .

By now many other **Lakotas**, who had heard the shooting, were coming up from Pine Ridge, and we all charged on the soldiers. They ran eastward toward where the trouble began. We followed down along the dry gulch, and what we saw was terrible. Dead and wounded women and children and little babies were scattered all along there where they had been trying to run away. The soldiers had followed along the gulch, as they ran, and murdered them in there. Sometimes they were in heaps because they had huddled together, and some were scattered all along. Sometimes bunches of them had been killed and torn to pieces where the wagon guns hit them. . . .

When I saw this I wished that I had died too, but I was not sorry for the women and children. It was better for them to be happy in the other world, and I wanted to be there too. But before I went there I wanted to have revenge. I thought there might be a day, and we should have revenge.

After the soldiers marched away, I heard from my friend, Dog Chief, how the trouble started, and he was right there by Yellow Bird when it happened. This is the way it was:

In the morning the soldiers began to take all the guns away from the **Big Foots**. . . . The people had stacked most of their guns, and even their knives, by the tepee where Big Foot was lying sick. Soldiers were on the little hill and all around, and there were soldiers across the dry gulch to the south and over east along Wounded Knee Creek too. The people were nearly surrounded, and the wagon-guns were pointing at them.

Some had not yet given up their guns, and so the soldiers were searching all the tepees, throwing things around and poking into everything. There was a man called Yellow Bird, and he and another man were standing in front of the tepee where Big Foot was lying sick. They had white sheets around and over them, with eyeholes to look through, and they had guns under these. An officer came to search them. He took the other man's gun, and then started to take Yellow Bird's. But Yellow Bird would not let go. He wrestled with the officer, and while they were wrestling, the gun went off and killed the officer. **Wasichus** and some others have said he meant to do this, but Dog Chief was standing right there, and he told me it was not so. As soon as the gun went off, Dog Chief told me, an officer shot and killed Big Foot who was lying sick inside the tepee.

Then suddenly nobody knew what was happening, except that the soldiers were all shooting and the wagon-guns began going off right in among the people.

Many were shot down right there. The women and children ran into the gulch and up west, dropping all the time, for the soldiers shot them as they ran.

There were only about a hundred warriors and there were nearly five hundred soldiers. The warriors rushed to where they had piled their guns and knives. They fought soldiers with only their hands until they got their guns. . . .

It was a good winter day when all this happened. The sun was shining. But after the soldiers marched away from their dirty work, a heavy snow began to fall. The wind came up in the night. There was a big blizzard, and it grew very cold. The snow drifted deep in the crooked gulch, and it was one long grave of **butchered** women and children and babies, who had never done any harm and were only trying to run away.

A rifle shot touched off the bloody battle between U.S. troops and the Sioux at Wounded Knee. This was the last of the big battles between Native Americans and U.S. soldiers.

Wounded Knee was the site of the last big battle between soldiers and Native Americans on the northern plains. Shortly after the battle a mighty blizzard covered the land. It froze the bodies of the Sioux who died there. Black Elk recalled the tragedy. He said, ". . . something else died there in the bloody mud and was buried in the blizzard. A people's dream died there. It was a beautiful dream."

A NEW CENTURY

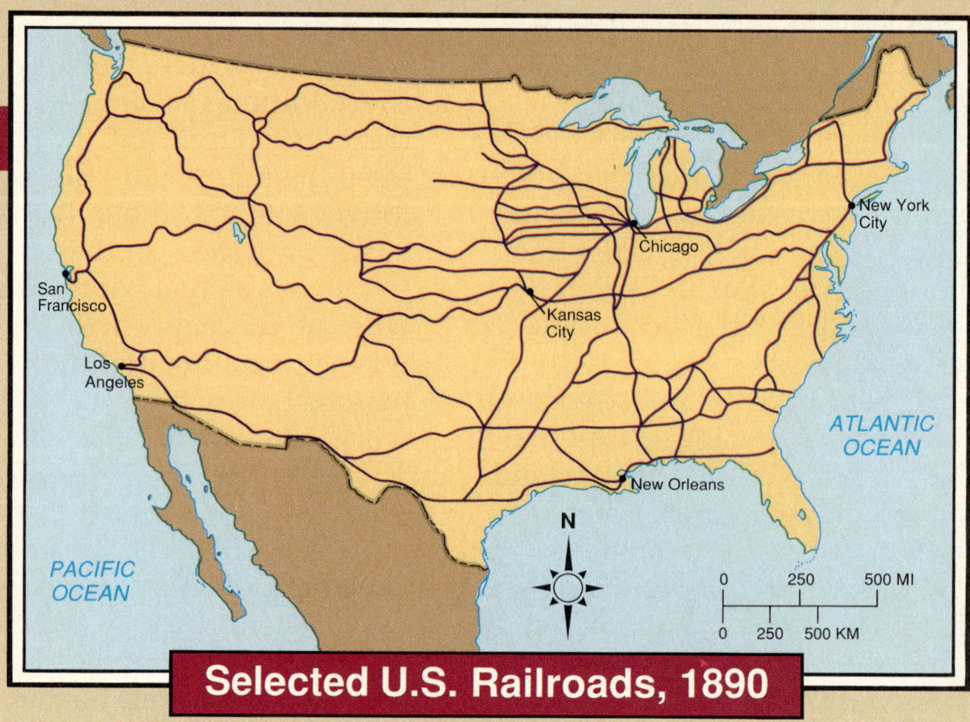

Selected U.S. Railroads, 1890

Civil War: the war between North and South in the United States (1861 to 1865)

mass production: making large quantities of an item using machines

transcontinental: cross-country

mail-order houses: businesses that sell goods through the mail

immigrants: people from one country who come to another country to live

The long and bloody **Civil War** was behind them. Now Americans could look to the future with hope. Industry was booming. While inventors created new machines, scientists found new sources of power. Businesses made more goods at lower prices using **mass production**. Better kinds of transportation, such as the **transcontinental** railroad, carried goods across the country. And department stores and **mail-order houses** helped every customer find what he or she needed.

This huge growth in industry created millions of new jobs. People in other countries heard about these jobs. Many of them came to the United States to work. From 1860 to 1920 more than 25 million **immigrants** came to the United States. They hoped to make a better life for themselves and their families.

But many business owners mistreated their workers. They made them work long hours for low pay in noisy, dirty factories. Workers were often injured because of unsafe working conditions. Often young children had to work to help their families earn enough money to live on.

1880	1885	1890

1880 Half a million people immigrate to the United States.

Workers began to band together in **labor unions**. As a group they could push for changes in the workplace. Some unions **went on strike** for more money and shorter hours. Later Congress passed laws to improve working conditions and wages.

Meanwhile, the size of the country grew too. The United States bought Alaska from Russia in 1867 and **annexed** Hawaii in 1898. Then the United States won the **Spanish-American War**. It gained control of the Philippines, Guam, and Puerto Rico.

By 1914 industry in the United States was doing well. And the United States had the military strength to win a foreign war. The country had gone through major changes since the end of the Civil War. Those changes helped to form the modern American nation.

In the early 1900s new forms of transportation linked major U.S. cities. Railroads, steamships, and a canal system made it easier to ship goods from one place to another.

In this unit three individuals share their experiences in a changing America.

- **Radie**, a Polish immigrant, tells about her new job and life in the United States.
- **Alfred Miller,** a mail-order customer, writes a letter to Sears, Roebuck and Co. to express his satisfaction with a product.
- **Theodore Roosevelt** describes the hardships he and his men faced in the Spanish-American War.

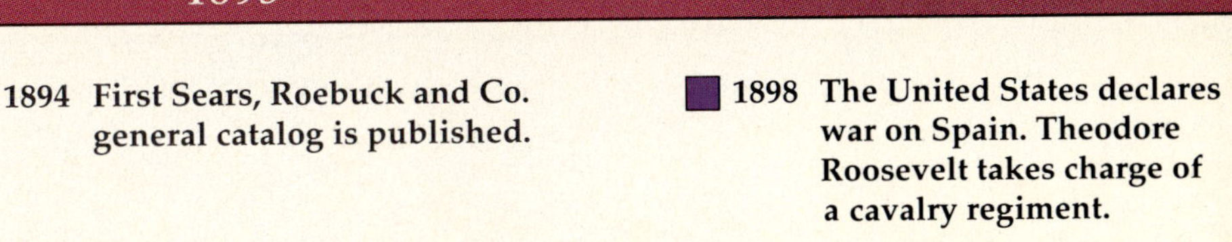

Sweatshop Girl

> " . . . I made $4 a week by working six days in the week. . . . "
>
> **Radie, a factory worker**

Photographer Lewis Hine took this picture of a woman working in a New York factory in the early 1900s.

In the late 1800s most immigrants to the United States came from southern and eastern Europe. Many were farmers who lost their land when crop prices fell. Others were Jews who had been mistreated because of their religious beliefs. Many immigrants had to work long hours in noisy, dirty factories under unsafe conditions. Such factories were called sweatshops. A Polish immigrant tells of her experience.

When mother died I thought I would try to learn a trade and then I could go to school at night and learn to speak the English language well.

So I went to work in Allen Street (Manhattan) in what they call a sweatshop, making skirts by machine. I was new at the work and the foreman scolded me a great deal.

"Now, then," he would say, "this place is not for you to be looking around in. Attend to your work. That is what you have to do."

I did not know at first that you must not look around and talk, and I made many mistakes with the sewing, so that I was often called a "stupid animal." But I made $4 a week by working six days in the week. . . .

I lived at this time with a girl named Ella, who worked in the same factory and made $5 a week. We had the room all to ourselves, paying $1.50 a week for it, and doing light housekeeping. It was in Allen Street, and the window looked out of the back, which was good, because there was an

1842

1842 U.S. government makes labor unions legal.

1877 Railroad workers strike across the United States.

1886 The American Federation of Labor, a national worker's union, is formed.

1890 The number of industrial workers climbs to over 3.2 million, up from 885,000 in 1860.

New York was home to millions of immigrants. Many immigrant families lived above stores in crowded one-room apartments with no heat or water.

elevated railroad in front, and in summer time a great deal of dust and dirt came in at the front windows. . . .

We did our cooking on an oil stove, and lived well, as this list of our expenses . . . will show:

ELLA AND RADIE FOR FOOD
(ONE WEEK)

Tea	$0.06
Cocoa	.10
Bread and rolls	.40
Canned vegetables	.20
Potatoes	.10
Milk	.21
Fruit	.20
Butter	.15
Meat	.60
Fish	.15
Laundry	.25
Total	$2.42
Add rent	1.50
Grand Total	$3.92

Of course, we could have lived cheaper, but we are both fond of good things and felt that we could afford them. . . .

It cost me $2 a week to live, and I had a $1 a week to spend on clothing and pleasure, and saved the other dollar. I went to night school, but it was hard work learning at first as I did not know much English.

Two years ago I came to this place, Brownsville, where so many of my people are, and where I have friends. I got work in a factory making **underskirts**—all sorts of cheap underskirts, like cotton and **calico** for the summer and woolen for the winter, but never the silk, satin, or velvet underskirts. I earned $4.50 a week and lived on $2 a week, the same as before.

I got a room in the house of some friends who lived near the

1924	

| **1900** Nearly nine million people immigrate to the United States during the next ten years. | **1911** A fire at a clothing factory kills 146 workers. Many states begin to pass anti-sweatshop laws. | **1924** Congress passes new laws to limit the number of immigrants from each country. |

factory. I pay $1 a week for the room and am allowed to do light housekeeping—that is, cook my meals in it. . . . My food for a week costs $1, just as it did in Allen Street, and I have the rest of my money to do as I like with. I am earning $5.50 a week now, and will probably get another increase soon.

It isn't **piecework** in our factory, but one is paid by the amount of work done just the same. So it is like piecework. All the **hands** get different amounts, some as low as $3.50 and some of the men as high as $16 a week. The factory is in the third story of a brick building. It is in a room twenty feet long and fourteen broad. There are fourteen machines in it. I and the daughter of the people with whom I live work two of these machines. The other operators are all men, some young and some old.

I get up at half-past five o'clock every morning and make myself a cup of coffee on the oil stove. I eat a bit of bread and perhaps some fruit and then go to work. Often I get there soon after six o'clock so as to be in good time, though the factory does not open till seven. I have heard that there is a sort of clock that calls you at the very time you want to get up, but I can't believe that because I don't see how the clock would know.

At seven o'clock we all sit down to our machines and the boss brings to each one the pile of work that he or she is to finish during the day, what they call in English their "stint." This pile is put down beside the machine and as soon as a skirt is done it is laid on the other side of the machine. Sometimes the work is not all finished by six o'clock and then

Before child-labor laws were passed, many young children worked in factories and coal mines. In this photo a young girl learns how to use a spinning machine in a textile factory.

the one who is behind must work overtime. Sometimes one is finished ahead of time and gets away at four or five o'clock, but generally we are not done till six o'clock.

The machines go like mad all day, because the faster you work the more money you get. Sometimes in my haste I get my finger caught and the needle goes right through it. It goes so quick, though, that it does not hurt much. I bind the finger up with a piece of cotton and go on working. We all have accidents like that. Where the needle goes through the nail it makes a sore finger, or where it splinters a bone it does much harm. Sometimes a finger has to come off. Generally, though, one can be cured by a **salve**. . . .

I am going back to night school again this winter. Plenty of my friends go there. Some of the women in my class are more than forty years of age. Like me, they did not have a chance to learn anything in the old country. It is good to have an education; it makes you feel higher. Ignorant people are all low. People say now that I am clever and fine in conversation.

We have just finished a strike in our business. It spread all over and the United Brotherhood of Garment Workers was in it. That takes in the cloakmakers, coat-makers, and all the others. We struck for shorter hours, and after being out four weeks won the fight. We only have to work nine and a half hours a day and we get the same pay as before. So the union does good after all in spite of what some people say against it—that it just takes our money and does nothing.

I pay 25 cents a month to the union, but I do not **begrudge** that because it is for our benefit. The next strike is going to be for a raise of wages. . . .

Some of the women blame me very much because I spend so much money on clothes. They say that instead of $1 a week I ought not to spend more than 25 cents a week on clothes, and that I should save the rest. . . . Those who blame me are the old-country people who have old-fashioned notions, but the people who have been here a long time know better. . . .

I have many friends and we often have jolly parties. . . .

Many women who worked in the sweatshops of New York joined forces to protest the poor working conditions.

New immigrants sometimes joined labor unions and risked their jobs by striking. But most immigrants were afraid to be without work in a strange country. They accepted low wages and owners' rules, and that angered many American-born workers. These workers demanded limits on immigration. In 1882 the government set limits for the first time on the number of new immigrants coming to the United States.

Mail-Order
America

A Satisfied Customer

The pages of the 1897 Sears catalog were
filled with low-priced merchandise.

In the late 1800s and early 1900s, merchants found new ways to sell their products. Sears, Roebuck and Co. was one of the first successful mail-order houses. Its catalogs were filled with pictures of merchandise that people could buy through the mail. Even people in small towns and rural areas could find the things they needed. The letter below is from one satisfied customer in Kentucky. It was written in 1897.

Messrs.:
abbreviation for
Messieurs, French
word meaning
gentlemen

phaeton: four-
wheel, horse-drawn
vehicle

hesitancy: doubt

Messrs. Sears, Roebuck & Co.,

Dear Sirs: Some time about the first of August, I ordered one **phaeton** No. 125, price $63.00, full leather top and back curtain, lamps and fenders left off. The buggy came all right and I have no **hesitancy** in saying that I have one of the best, neatest and easiest riding buggies, and everyone that rides in it says the same thing. I think the same vehicle would cost about $80.00 or $85.00, some say it would cost $100.00. It comes fully up to my expectations and I am well pleased with my bargain.

Respectfully your friend,
Alfred Miller

1886		1925
1886 Richard W. Sears starts a mail-order watch company in Minneapolis.	**1887** Sears hires Alvah C. Roebuck to repair watches. **1893** Sears, Roebuck and Co. is founded.	**1894** First Sears, Roebuck and Co. general catalog is published. **1925** The first Sears, Roebuck and Co. retail store opens.

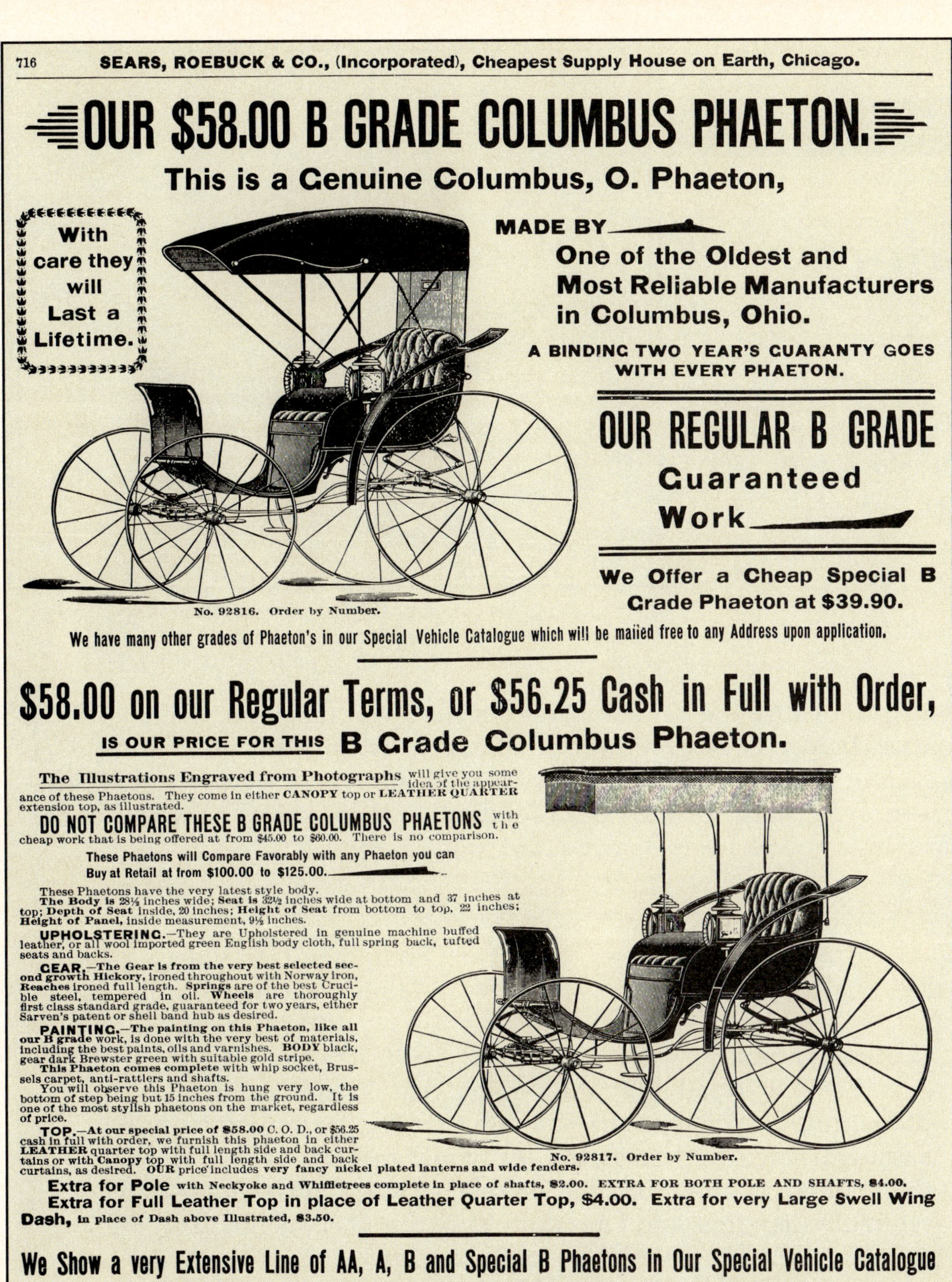

Mr. Miller ordered a horse-drawn wagon from the Sears catalog. Many farmers and their families used the catalog to do their shopping.

With the great success of its mail-order business, Sears, Roebuck and Co. began to branch out. In 1925 Sears opened the doors of its first retail store in Chicago. Today Sears has hundreds of department stores, but it is still in the mail-order business. Each year the company distributes more than 300 million catalogs.

From *1897 Sears Roebuck Catalogue*, by permission of Sears, Roebuck and Co. Excerpt from p. 772.

Rough Riders in Cuba

❝ The suffering has been hideous. . . . **❞**

Theodore Roosevelt

Before leaving his camp for the Spanish-American War, Theodore Roosevelt wrote a letter to his sister.

In April of 1898 the United States declared war on Spain. United States soldiers helped Cubans fight for freedom from Spanish rule. Future president Theodore Roosevelt left his desk job with the Navy to become an officer in charge of a cavalry regiment. In these letters he writes of the hardships he and his men faced. ✍

Anna: Anna Roosevelt Cowles, Theodore Roosevelt's sister

dismounted: without their horses

Will: Anna's husband

First Regt. U.S. Vol. Cavalry,
In Camp near Tampa, Fla.
June 7th, 1898.

Darling **Anna**:

We hope to sail tonight for Cuba, that is, eight troops **dismounted**. We do not like having to leave the remainder and having to leave our horses, but we would rather crawl on all fours than not go. I don't think that there ever was a more interesting regiment than this, and I am quite sure that there is not in all the world a regiment to which I would so soon belong.

. . . I am awfully busy, and I owe it to a chance that I am able to send you this letter.

With best love to **Will**.

Ever faithfully yours,
Theodore Roosevelt.

Feb. 1898			
Feb. 1898 An explosion blows up the American battleship *Maine* in the Havana, Cuba, harbor.	**Apr. 1898** The United States declares war on Spain. Theodore Roosevelt takes charge of a cavalry regiment.	**May 1898** The U.S. Navy destroys the Spanish fleet in the Philippines.	

On Board U.S. Transport *Yucatan*
Port Tampa, Fla.
June 12, 1898.

Darling **Bye**,

This is our sixth day **sweltering** on this troop ship under the semi-tropical sun in **Tampa** harbor. It is not a large ship and has a thousand men aboard. We have given up the decks to the men, so that the officers are confined to the cabin, but even so it is far easier for us than for them. If the authorities in their wisdom keep us much longer in this ship, we shall certainly have some **epidemic** of disease. Why . . . we should have been put on the **transports** before sailing I cannot tell. . . .

The delay is most irritating and the **enforced idleness** and crowding **tells on** the **morale** of the men. Nevertheless, they have stood it astonishingly well and taken it in very good part so far. . . .

Ever yours,
Theodore Roosevelt.

Bye: nickname for Anna

sweltering: suffering in the heat

Tampa: Florida port city on the Gulf of Mexico

epidemic: rapidly spreading

transports: ships used to carry troops or supplies

enforced idleness: time spent doing nothing

tells on: affects

morale: state of mind

Theodore Roosevelt (center, with glasses) formed a cavalry unit called the *Rough Riders* to fight the Spanish-American War. Many men left their jobs to join the war.

Aug. 1898

July 1898   Roosevelt leads his Rough Riders to victory near Santiago, Cuba.

Aug. 1898   The Spanish-American War ends.

Santiago
July 19th, '98.

Darling Bye:

I was very glad to get your letter. Any underclothes and socks and at present trousers and shoes; and above all, any **delicacies** like chocolate, canned fruit, canned meats of good quality, rice and oatmeal, would be **immensely** appreciated. What my men need most, that can be sent, is enough food and clothing. We need still more, hospital supplies and above all, transportation, (I suppose it has been the lack of the **latter** that has prevented the Red Cross, which has done good work, from sending the **former**); but these I fear must be furnished by the government. . . . We can't use **hammocks**—there are too many men and we can't get poles from which to hang them. After a fight or a late march, we just sleep anywhere, often without even a blanket; in a more permanent camp we build little bunks on poles raised on bars across crotched sticks.

The **mismanagement** of the transportation, and hospital services has been beyond belief. The wounded lie in the mud on **sodden** blankets; some of my men went *forty-eight* hours without food after being sent to the hospital. The attendance has been bad; and above all, they have had no proper food and but little medicine. I have had to buy from my own pocket rice and oatmeal and **condensed milk** for my sick men and beans and cornmeal and sugar for the wornout hungry fighters who were still able to dig in the trenches. It is small wonder that of the 600 men with whom I landed, today over 300 are dead or in hospital from wounds and disease. . . . The utter lack of **executive** ability . . . , both at Washington and here, are responsible for it all. . . .

The suffering has been **hideous**; and at least half of it was **readily** avoidable. There have been practically no supplies at the front save **hardtack**, bacon and coffee; and for men in high fever such **fare** is not good.

My own health has been good; and I would not have missed this for anything, even were I to die tomorrow. . . . It is a great regiment; and I have done with it all that could be done. . . .

Ever yours,
T.R.

Santiago
July 22nd, 1898.

Dear **Douglas**,

Will you send Samuel MacMillan, the former Park Commissioner, 100 dollars? I borrowed it to get food for the Regiment, having used up $300 of my own for the same purpose; only thus have I been able to keep them in the **indifferent** health in which they are. I also got some food from the Red Cross for them, which was greatly appreciated— rice, corn meal, condensed milk, oatmeal. What we need is food and clothing; and the only way to get it is for me to buy it, until there is a chance to send us more, now there is none.

. . . Meanwhile, I'll use **any** I can **draw** or borrow for myself and if I am not **reimbursed**, why it doesn't matter. Half of my men are dead, wounded or down with fever.

Yours always,
Theodore Roosevelt.

indifferent: neither good nor bad

any: money

draw: get or receive

reimbursed: paid back

Santiago
July 28th, '98.

Darling Bye,

A lot of Red Cross things have come, **presumably** from you, and they are most useful—soups, malted milk, prunes, etc., for the sick and even a little for the well, soap and underclothes, socks and towels. . . . Do thank everyone. The Red Cross has done a great deal for this regiment, and we deeply appreciate it.

We are now in a permanent camp, and my men at last have plenty of food, after a month's semi-starvation and **intolerable** hardship and labor, and in a day or two they will have clothes and **tentage**, I think. Now the hammocks would be useful, at least to some extent. Some of the men are using them, but with **dog tents** it is almost impossible to swing them, and it is difficult for ten thousand men camped together to get proper poles.

As for me, I have been in good health throughout. . . . This has **enabled** me in time of need to do and **endure** everything and so far I have not been an hour off duty.

I can hardly say how proud I am of this regiment. It is so typically American! It is just the ideal **body** for me to lead; and the men are devoted to me, and in the field I can lead and handle them as I think no other man could. . . .

Yours always,
T.R.

presumably: I assume

intolerable: too hard or painful to bear

tentage: tents

dog tents: small tents for two people

enabled: made it possible for

endure: put up with

body: group

The United States defeated the Spanish within four months. Roosevelt's men faced sickness and food shortages. But still they helped to win the important battle of San Juan Hill. Roosevelt's regiment was often called the Rough Riders, a popular nickname for cowboys. Roosevelt's fame as an officer helped him win the vice-presidential election in 1900.

A WORLD IN CONFLICT

Europe in the First World War

alliances: agreements among nations to help each other protect their common interests

Serbia: a country in the Balkans, now part of Yugoslavia

allies: members of the same alliance

neutral: not joining a side in a war

Allied Powers: the nations that fought Germany in WWI

Central Powers: the nations that helped Germany in WWI

In the early 1900s the European powers set up a system of **alliances**. These alliances helped to protect countries from attack. For example, Germany, Austria-Hungary, and Italy agreed to help each other if Russia attacked any of them. In 1914 the shooting of an Austrian prince was the first of several events that led to war. First Austria-Hungary declared war on **Serbia**. Then nation after nation joined the war to help their **allies.** World War I had begun.

Most Americans believed that the United States had no place in the war in Europe. President Woodrow Wilson said that the United States would remain **neutral**. However, American feeling soon turned against Germany. Germany invaded neutral Belgium. Germany sank a British passenger ship and three American ships. In April 1917 Congress declared war on Germany. The United States joined World War I on the side of the **Allied Powers.** The government built up support for the war effort. Posters and songs encouraged young men to join the army.

With help from the United States, the Allied Powers defeated the **Central Powers** by November of 1918. But victory came at a

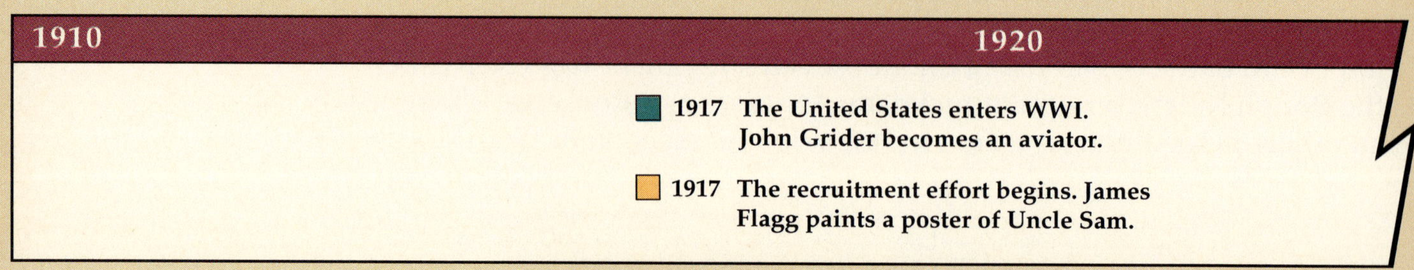

high price. More than 110,000 American troops were killed. At least 230,000 were wounded. In all nearly ten million soldiers died in World War I.

The 1920s were good years for most Americans. The war was over. Jobs were plentiful. Industry produced new inventions such as cars, refrigerators, and vacuum cleaners. These products made life easier. People had more time to do things for fun.

But in 1929 the New York stock market crashed. Banks and people with savings lost large sums of money. People bought fewer goods. Many companies went out of business. By 1933 about one quarter of the nation's workers were out of work. The United States was in the midst of the **Great Depression**. When President Franklin D. Roosevelt took office in 1933, he began to work at solving these problems by beginning his **New Deal** program.

Great Depression: the period (1929–1940) during which U.S. business dropped sharply

New Deal: President Roosevelt's plan to end the depression through new government programs

During the Great Depression people without jobs lined up at soup kitchens for free meals.

In this unit several individuals describe the United States in the first half of the twentieth century.

- The diary of **John M. Grider** reveals his experiences as a pilot for the United States in World War I.
- In his autobiography **James M. Flagg** describes how he created the Uncle Sam poster to encourage people to join the military.
- Letters to **President and Mrs. Roosevelt** from unemployed workers and their families describe their desperate situation during the Great Depression.

1930

1940

- **1935** Ten million Americans are unemployed. Franklin Roosevelt gives Americans hope with his New Deal program.

War Birds

> **❝** . . . I am going to have the opportunity to die as every brave man should wish to die—fighting . . . for my country. . . . **❞**
>
> **John MacGavock Grider**

The airplane was a new weapon in World War I.

John MacGavock Grider was a 25-year-old farmer in Arkansas when the United States declared war on Germany. Grider volunteered for service and was sent to England to train as a pilot. He began to keep a diary on his way across the Atlantic aboard a British steamship. In the diary Grider wrote about the adventure and the destruction of war. ∞

R.M.S.: Royal Mail Steamship

Halifax: capital of Canadian province of Nova Scotia

convoy: ships traveling in a group for protection

aviators: pilots

embryo: early stage of development

privates: soldiers of the lowest rank

Captain La Guardia: member of U.S. House of Representatives who became mayor of New York City

September 20th, 1917

Aboard **R.M.S.** *Carmania* in the harbor of **Halifax**.

Well, here I am aboard ship and three days out of New York, waiting for a **convoy** at Halifax. This seems to be a fitting place to start a diary. I am leaving my continent as well as my country and am going forth in search of adventure, which I hope to find in Italy, for that is where we are headed. We are a hundred and fifty **aviators** in **embryo** commanded by Major MacDill, who is an officer and a gentleman in fact as well as by Act of Congress.

We are traveling first class, thanks to him, tho we are really only **privates**, and every infantry officer on board hates our guts because we have the same privileges they do. . . .

My platoon is assigned to the top deck and **Captain La Guardia** is in charge of our boat. He is a congressman from New York City and learned to fly last year. He is an Italian so was sent over with us. . . .

I probably won't write much in this thing. I never have done anything constantly except the wrong thing, but I want a few

<table>
<tr><td colspan="3">Apr. 1917</td></tr>
<tr>
<td>Apr. 1917 President Wilson asks Congress to declare war on Germany.</td>
<td>Sept. 1917 John Grider, volunteer pilot trainee, boards a ship for Europe.</td>
<td>May 1918 Grider completes training and is assigned to the British Air Force.</td>
</tr>
</table>

recollections jotted down in case I don't get killed.

. . . I don't want to be a hero—too often they are all clay from the feet up, but I want to die as a man should. Thank God, I am going to have the opportunity to die as every brave man should wish to die—fighting—and fighting for my country as well. That would **retrieve** my wasted years and **neglected** opportunities.

But if I don't get killed, I want to be able to jog my memory in my **declining** years so I can say, "Back in 1917 when I was an aviator, I used to—!" . . .

October 3rd

So this is England. We landed yesterday morning and took a train right at the dock for **Oxford**. We aren't going to Italy after all.

We've got to go to **Ground School** all over again. Our orders got all bawled up in Paris and MacDill, La Guardia, the doctors, the enlisted men and Spalding have gone on to France. MacDill said he would go on to Paris and get the orders straightened out and come back for us. Somebody had made a mistake. All our mail is in Italy, all our money is in **lira** and our letters of credit are drawn on banks in Rome and we've wasted two weeks studying Italian and two months going to Ground School learning nonsense for now we've got to go thru this British Ground School here. . . .

October 8th

I hear that the Germans have the goods in airplanes and **A.A. guns**. . . . Of course, no one doubts

recollections: memories

retrieve: make up for

neglected: missed, overlooked

declining: last

Oxford: city in England about 50 miles northwest of London

Ground School: school in which future pilots learn how to fly airplanes

lira: unit of money in Italy

A.A. guns: antiaircraft guns used to defend against enemy air attacks

Before a pilot stepped into the cockpit of a war plane, he had to go through many hours of special training on the ground.

Nov. 1918

June 1918 Grider is killed during air combat. Elliot Springs continues his diary.

Nov. 1918 Germany surrenders to the Allies.

our winning out in the end but it will be a long hard fight and few of us will be left to enjoy the fruits of our victory. I surely am lucky not to be in the **trenches**. Some, in fact, most of the cadets have been out and they say it's hell. "Only we young chaps can stand it," they say. . . .

October 19th

A British major with the **D.S.O.** and the **M.C.** talked to us the other day. He said as I remember it,

"You men are starting on a long trip. It's a hard trip and will require a lot of courage. You'll all be frightened many times but most of you will be able to conquer your fear and carry on. But if you find that fear has gotten the best of you and you can't **stick it** and you are **beyond bucking up**, don't go on and cause the death of brave men thru your failure. Quit where you are and try something else. Courage is needed above all else. If five of you meet five **Huns** and one of you is yellow and doesn't

do his part and lets the others down, the four others will be killed thru the failure of the one and maybe that one himself.

"This individual hero stuff is all **tommy rot**. It's devotion to duty and **concerted** effort and disciplined team work that will win the war.

"War is cruel, war is senseless and war is a **plague**, but we've got to win it and there's no better use of your life than to give it to help stop this eternal slaughter.

"It's a war of men—strong determined men and weaklings have no part in it."

He looked just like he talked.

None of the men I've talked to curse the Hun particularly. So far, I've met no eye witnesses of **atrocities** and not much is said of them. . . .

November 18th

I went to Stokes Castle this afternoon for lunch and stayed for tea. I think this has been the best day I have spent in England. I met a Mrs. Chapin out there from

Some soldiers fought in trenches for months at a time. These ditches, lined with sandbags, were often muddy, cold, and a haven to disease-carrying rats.

Louisiana. She is a sure-enough Southern **aristocrat** and I am proud of her. She reminded me of Gramma. She **dominated** the whole table at dinner and was so interesting and made every one feel at home. She took me to her room and showed me the picture of her old home in Louisiana. It was an old Italian **villa** on the banks of the Mississippi. I certainly enjoyed talking to her. It was like a visit home. I wonder if I will ever see the Mississippi again. . . .

We leave for **Thetford** to-morrow at eight-thirty and at last I am really going to learn to fly. It's over six months since I **enlisted** to fly and I am not sorry they are past. . . .

November 25th

To-day I saw my first **scout machine**, a **Sopwith Pup**. It's the prettiest little thing I ever laid my eyes on. I am going to fly one if I live long enough. They aren't as big as a minute and are as pretty and slick as a thoroughbred horse. Tiny little things, just big enough for one man and a machine gun. . . .

December 6th

I have been flying for three days and Capt. Harrison says I can **solo** to-morrow if it's calm. I tell you it's a great life. I am absolutely ruined for anything else. I wish I could describe it. The thing most surprising to me is the feeling of absolute safety. I have put in two hours and twenty minutes in the air and I would have soloed this evening if it had been calm enough. . . .

February 9th

A horrible thing happened to-day. We were all out on the

In this painting by Kenneth McDonough a British biplane sweeps down on its morning patrol in France.

tarmac having our pictures taken for **posterity** when somebody yelled and pointed up. Two **Avros** collided right over the **airdrome** at about three thousand feet. . . . It was a horrible sight. We didn't know who was in either one of them. I was glad I was sitting next to Cal. They came down in a slow spin with their wings locked together and both of them in flames. Fred Stillman was in one machine and got out alive but badly burned and Doug Ellis was in the other one and was burned to a cinder. . . .

May 14th

All aboard for France. Our orders have come thru and we leave next Wednesday. . . .

June 8th

This morning I arose at three-thirty—two-thirty real time—and by six I was back for breakfast and the Huns had wasted a thousand pounds' worth of **Archie shells** on us. Our hands might have been a

Germany and the United States were
shown as fighting birds on this
recruitment poster.

bit steadier as we raised a coffee
cup, but a little exposure to the
hate of the Hun does give you a
wonderful appetite. . . .

Again at eleven I went out to
do battle. We got into a **dogfight**
over **Ostend** and had a merry
little **fracas**.

I was up above the main
formation to see that nothing
dropped down out of the sun and
a **Pfaltz dove** on me. He came
right out of the sun but I've
learned to put my thumb up and
close one eye and unless they are
at a dead angle, I can see them. I
saw this one in time and just as he
opened fire, I turned quickly and
threw his sights off. His **tracer** was
going a hundred feet behind my
tail. The Hun went on by and half
rolled onto my tail. I kept turning
to keep his sights off me and he
followed. We turned around and
around—each **maneuvering** to get
into position to fire a burst at close
range. But I had learned my lesson
well at **Ayr** and I could do perfect
vertical banks and I began gain-
ing on him. I was getting in posi-

tion to open up when he half
rolled to break away. I half rolled
after him and was on his tail like a
hawk after a chicken. I let him
have both guns at close range. My
sights were dead on his **cockpit**
and I must have got in about a
hundred and fifty **rounds**. My
Lewis jammed after fifty rounds
but my **Vickers** kept going. The
Hun started to turn, then he
flopped over on his back and went
straight down. He was last seen
headed towards his future home
and breaking all records—hell
bent for **hades**! I couldn't see him
crash so I only got an "out of
control." But I know I got him. At
the speed he was diving he never
could have pulled out. And I
know now that I can fight as well
as fly. . . .

---

*John Grider was killed in air
combat on June 18, 1918. Before he
was shot down he gave his diary to his
closest friend, Elliot Springs. Springs
added his own entries describing the
events of July and August.*

July 28th
I can't write much these days.
I'm too nervous. I can hardly hold
a pen. I'm all right in the air, as
calm as a cucumber, but on the
ground I'm a wreck and I get
panicky. . . .

August 27th
Many things have happened.
I hear that Bobby got shot down
up at **Dunkirk** and is no more.
Tommy Herbert has been shot in
the rear with a **phosphorus** bullet.
Leach has been shot thru the
shoulder and isn't expected to pull
thru. Explosive bullet. Read is
dead and so is Molly Shaw.

Alex Mathews is dead. . . .

We've lost a lot of good men. It's only a question of time until we all get it. I'm all shot to pieces. I only hope I can stick it. I don't want to quit. My nerves are all gone and I can't stop. I've lived beyond my time already.

. . . Here I am, twenty-four years old, I look forty and I feel ninety. I've lost all interest in life beyond the next patrol. No one Hun will ever get me and I'll never fall into a trap, but sooner or later I'll be forced to fight against odds that are too long or perhaps a stray shot from the ground will be lucky and I will have **gone in vain**. Or my motor will cut out when we are **trench straffing** or a wing will pull off in a dive. Oh, for a parachute! The Huns are using them now. I haven't a chance, I know, and it's this eternal waiting around that's killing me. . . .

No date

War is a horrible thing, a **grotesque** comedy. And it is so useless. This war won't prove anything. . . .

It gives me a dizzy feeling every time I hear of the men that are gone. And they have gone so fast I can't keep track of them; every time two pilots meet it is only to swap news of who's killed. When a person takes sick, lingers in bed a few days, dies and is buried on the third day, it all

Crowds gathered to welcome home soldiers from the war. The war ended November 11, 1918, the day now known as Veterans Day.

seems regular and they pass on into the great beyond in an orderly manner and you accept their departure as an accomplished fact. But when you lunch with a man, talk to him, see him go out and get in his plane in the **prime** of his youth and the next day someone tells you that he is dead—it just doesn't sink in and you can't believe it. And the oftener it happens the harder it is to believe. I've lost over a hundred friends, so they tell me,—I've seen only seven or eight killed—but to me they aren't dead yet. They are just around the corner, I think, and I'm still expecting to run into them any time.

gone in vain: died without success

trench straffing: (strafing) firing machine guns into trenches from low-flying planes

grotesque: strange, twisted

prime: most active period

World War I ended in November 1918, and Elliot Springs returned to the United States. He published John Grider's diary in 1926. Grider Air Field in Arkansas was named for John Grider in 1941.

From *War Birds: Diary of an Unknown Aviator*, ed. Elliott White Springs (College Station: Texas A&M University Press, 1988). Excerpts from pp. 9–14, 24–25, 31–37, 54–57, 75, 138–39, 178–83, 236, 239, 263, 267–71.

Uncle Sam Wants You

James Montgomery Flagg

Artist James Montgomery Flagg used himself as a model for his famous "I Want You" recruitment poster.

Uncle Sam is a make-believe person created during the War of 1812. In that war some supplies given to soldiers were stamped with the letters "U.S." People began to say that the supplies were sent by "Uncle Sam," meaning the United States government. Artist James Montgomery Flagg made the most famous portrait of Uncle Sam during World War I. Below he tells how the government asked him to create his famous poster.

service: military

War Department: former name of U.S. Defense Department

Leslie's Weekly: weekly magazine

attend: take care of

recruiting posters: posters encouraging people to join the military

draft: system to select people for military service

this war: WWII

I was extremely active in 1917 in poster designing and in motion pictures for the **service**. I . . . made the first poster of the war. . . .

A man from the **War Department** in Washington called on me at my studio and showed me a sketch of Uncle Sam pointing at you with the caption, "I Want You!"

"Is that familiar to you?" he asked.

I said it was—that it was a poor copy of a cover I had made for *Leslie's Weekly*.

"Um, I thought so," he said, "this feller had 'em sold on his 'original' idea down at the War Department, but in the back of my head I knew I had seen it somewhere. I'll **attend** to this gent!"

So my original drawing was found, and from it they printed four million **recruiting posters**; this was, of course, before the **draft** and it is generally recognized as the most famous poster of that war. . . . The government printed 350,000 copies for recruiting for **this war**, . . . and about a million more for other purposes.

I didn't like the circusy Uncle Sam with stars all over him so I made a new type: a handsome, dignified figure. . . .

1914		1918
1914 World War I begins.	**1917 The United States enters World War I.**	**1918 World War I ends.**

Most Americans wanted the United States to stay out of World War I. Flagg's colorful posters were put in store windows and post offices to spark interest in the war effort.

Flagg had many talents as an artist. He was a magazine illustrator and a well-known painter. He wrote 24 silent films and his autobiography. Flagg died in New York City in 1960. In 1961 Congress made Flagg's figure of Uncle Sam a national symbol.

From James Montgomery Flagg, *Roses and Buckshot* (New York: G.P. Putnam's Sons, 1946), pp. 156–58. Reprinted by permission of Faith Flagg.

Letters to the Roosevelts

Writer unknown

When President Franklin Roosevelt and his wife Eleanor moved into the White House, more than 15 million people were jobless.

The Great Depression was a time of much human suffering. Millions of people lost their savings and their jobs. They had little money for food, clothing, and shelter. Thousands lost their homes. People everywhere wrote to their new president and first lady, Franklin and Eleanor Roosevelt, for help. In the week that followed Roosevelt's **inauguration**, 450,000 letters were sent to the White House.

inauguration: formal service or ceremony that marks the beginning of a term of office

of: from

Handcock: Hancock Insurance Company

where: (wear)

bot: (about)

September 15, 1935

Dear President

I have written to you before, It is worse than it was before I can not get a job and my mothers shop is not doing well pretty soon she will be laid off

Dear President we had to borrow money **of** my mother's policy the amount was $75 off of **Handcock** our insurance to pay taxes

Dear President Winter is coming and we have no coal I haven't got a suit of clothes, to **where** to church I hope you will give me a good answer and may God Bless you and Family You see I am the only boy and I am worried **bot** my mother   I don't want to lose her I hope you won't forget me.

Good Bye

My address is Jefferson Street, Troy, N.Y.

1929

1929	The stock market crashes. Panicked stockholders sell a record number of shares. The Depression begins.	1932	Franklin Delano Roosevelt is elected president.	1933	Unemployment climbs to 13 million. About 25 percent of the nation's workers are unemployed.

[February, 1936]

Mr. and Mrs. Roosevelt.
Wash. D.C.
Dear Mr. President:

    I'm a boy of 12 years. I want to tell you about my family   My father hasn't worked for 5 months   He went plenty times to **relief**, he filled out application. They won't give us anything. I don't know why. Please you do something. We haven't paid 4 months rent, Everyday the landlord rings the door bell, we don't open the door for him. We are afraid that **will** be put out, been put out before, and don't want to happen again. We haven't paid the gas bill, and the electric bill, haven't paid grocery bill for 3 months. My brother goes to Lane Tech. High School. he's eighteen years old, hasn't gone to school for 2 weeks because he got no carfare. I have a sister she's twenty years, she can't find work. My father he staying home. All the time he's crying because he can't find work. I told him why are you crying daddy, and daddy said why shouldn't I cry when there is nothing in the house. I feel sorry for him. That night I couldn't sleep. The next morning I wrote this letter to you. in my room. **Were** American citizens and were born in Chicago, Ill. and I don't know why they don't help us Please answer right away because we need it. **will** starve Thank you.

God bless you.
[Writer unknown]
Chicago, Ill.

relief: a government agency that provides aid for the poor

will: (we'll)

were: (we're)

will: (we'll)

The Roosevelts received about 6,500 letters a day during their stay at the White House. Fifty staff members were hired to answer the letters promptly. Roosevelt often read and signed the letters himself. Never before had Americans felt so strongly that their president cared about the common worker. Roosevelt's New Deal gave relief to the poor and unemployed. But the Great Depression did not end until 1942, after the United States had entered World War II.

From *Down and Out in the Great Depression: Letters from the "Forgotten Man"* edited by Robert S. McElvaine. © 1983 The University of North Carolina Press, pp. 117, 164. Reprinted by permission.

1944

1936 Roosevelt is re-elected to a second term as president.

1940 Roosevelt is re-elected to a third term as president.

1941 Unemployment rate is 15 percent. The United States enters World War II.

1944 Unemployment drops to 1 percent. Roosevelt is re-elected to a fourth term as president.

BIG WAR, LITTLE BATTLES

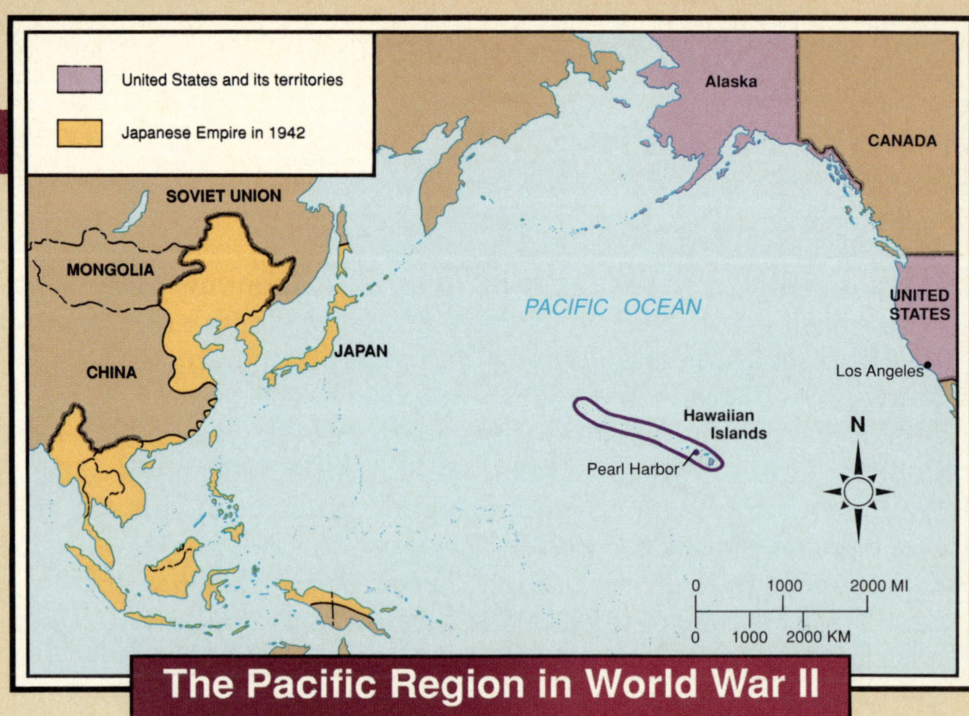

The Pacific Region in World War II

Adolf Hitler: leader of Germany from 1933 to 1945

alliance: an agreement among nations to protect their common interests

Allied Powers: the United States, Great Britain, China, the Soviet Union, and 46 other countries

Axis Powers: Germany, Italy, Japan, and six other countries

allies: countries that agree to help each other

In the 1930s Americans did not want to fight another war. They remembered how terrible World War I had been. But by 1940 Americans were alarmed by German, Italian, and Japanese actions. **Adolf Hitler's** German armies had taken over Czechoslovakia, Poland, Denmark, Norway, and Belgium. They invaded France, Yugoslavia, Greece, and the Soviet Union. Meanwhile, Japanese armies had invaded China. Japan also took over countries in southeast Asia and the Pacific.

Great Britain, France, and Russia were partners in an **alliance**. They were known as the **Allied Powers**. In 1940 Germany, Italy, and Japan also formed an alliance. They became known as the **Axis Powers.** Americans hoped the Allied Powers would defeat the Axis Powers. The United States started sending the Allied Powers tanks, ships, and weapons. It also refused to sell oil to Japan.

On December 7, 1941, Japanese fighter pilots attacked United States Navy ships in Pearl Harbor, Hawaii. The United States quickly declared war on Japan. Japan's **allies,** Germany and Italy, then declared war on the United States. The war raged for three and a half more years. As men went off to fight, women went to

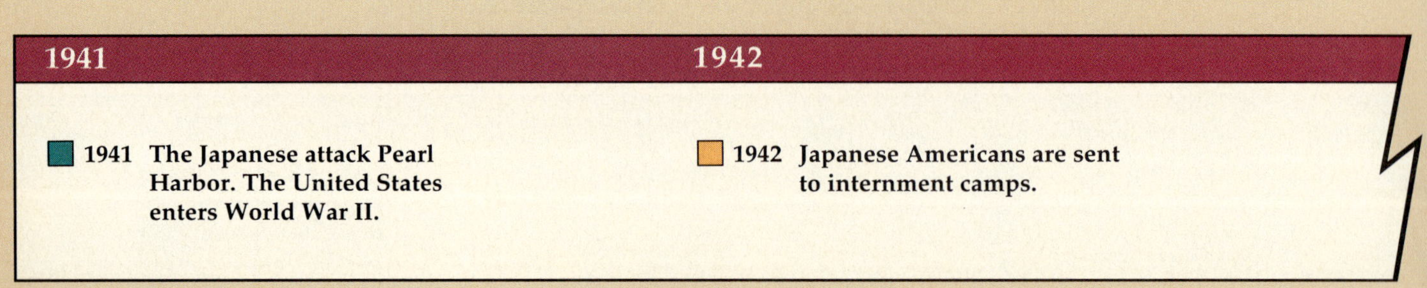

work in the factories. They helped to make planes, trucks, and other military goods. People tried not to waste supplies needed for the war. Students helped collect metal, rubber, and rags for the war effort. Goods that were scarce were **rationed**.

Finally the Allied Powers defeated the German army. On May 7, 1945, the German leaders surrendered. In August the United States dropped atomic bombs on the Japanese cities of Hiroshima and Nagasaki. The Japanese surrendered.

In World War II the United States built thousands of war planes to bomb German cities and factories.

The story of World War II is one of death and despair. The war affected everyone in some way. This unit contains the stories of three people. They describe what the war meant for them.

- In an interview **John Garcia** describes the event that led the United States into war.
- **Margaret Takahashi** tells in an interview how the lives of Japanese Americans were affected by the war.
- In a letter **President Harry Truman** announces the end of the war in Europe.

1943	1944	1945

1945 World War II ends.

An Eyewitness at Pearl Harbor

John Garcia

Naval yard workers scrambled to put out fires on the battleships anchored in Pearl Harbor.

On December 7, 1941, Japan made a surprise air attack on the United States. Japanese planes bombed U.S. ships anchored in Pearl Harbor, Hawaii. The United States suffered great losses. More than 2,000 people were killed. Eight battleships were sunk or badly damaged. More than 140 planes were destroyed. In this interview, witness John Garcia describes the events that plunged the United States into World War II.

apprentice: someone who learns a trade by helping a worker skilled in that trade

anti-aircraft: shells designed to defend against aircraft attacks

floating dry dock: a dock that can be put underwater to allow a ship to dock and then be raised to lift the ship from the water for repairs

I was sixteen years old, employed as a pipe fitter **apprentice** at Pearl Harbor Navy Yard. On December 7, 1941, oh, around 8:00 A.M., my grandmother woke me. She informed me that the Japanese were bombing Pearl Harbor. I said, "They're just practicing." She said, no, it was real and the announcer is requesting that all Pearl Harbor workers report to work. I went out on the porch and I could see the **anti-aircraft** fire up in the sky. I just said, "Oh boy."

I was four miles away. I got out on my motorcycle and it took me five, ten minutes to get there. It was a mess.

I was working on the U.S.S. *Shaw.* It was on a **floating dry dock.** It was in flames. I started to go down into the pipe fitter's shop to get my toolbox when another wave of Japanese came in. I got under a set of concrete steps at the dry dock where the battleship *Pennsylvania* was. An officer came by and asked me to go into the *Pennsylvania* and try to get the fires out. . . . I said, "There ain't no way I'm gonna go down there." It could blow up any minute. I was

<table>
<tr><td colspan="3">Dec. 7, 1941 6:00 A.M.</td></tr>
<tr>
<td>6:00 A.M. Japanese aircraft leave carriers for the flight to Pearl Harbor.</td>
<td>7:02 A.M. The U.S. Army notices Japanese aircraft on its radar but disregards.</td>
<td>7:55 A.M. The first bombs are dropped on Pearl Harbor.</td>
</tr>
</table>

young and sixteen, not stupid, not at sixty-two cents an hour. . . .

I was asked by some other officer to go into the water and get sailors out that had been blown off the ships. Some were unconscious, some were dead. So I spent the rest of the day swimming inside the harbor, along with some other Hawaiians. I brought out I don't know how many bodies and how many were alive and how many dead. Another man would put them into ambulances and they'd be gone. We worked all day at that. . . .

The following morning, I went with my tools to the *West Virginia*. It had **turned turtle**, totally upside down. We found a number of men inside. The *Arizona* was a total washout. Also the *Utah*. There were men in there, too. We spent about a month cutting the **superstructure** of the *West Virginia*, tilting it back on its **hull**. About three hundred men we cut out of there were still alive by the eighteenth day. . . . It took two weeks to get all the fires out. We worked around the clock for three days. There was so much excitement and confusion. . . .

When I came back after the third day, they told me that a shell had hit the house of my girl. We had been going together for, oh, about three years. Her house was a few blocks from my place. At the time, they said it was a Japanese bomb. Later we learned it was an American shell. She was killed. She was preparing for church at the time.

My neighbors met me. They were mostly Japanese. We all started to cry. We had no idea what was happening, what was going to happen. . . .

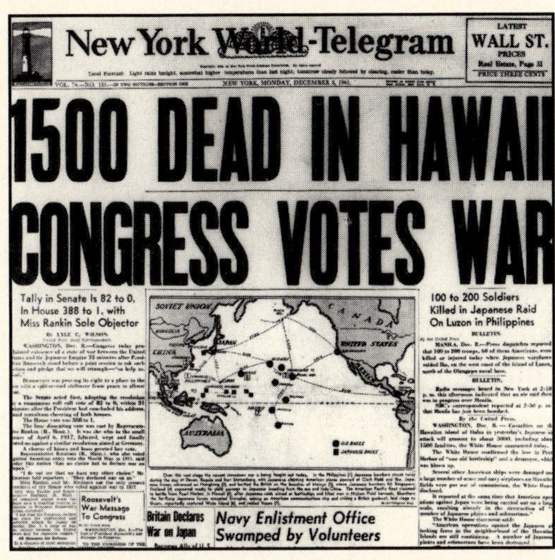

The day after the Pearl Harbor attack, newspapers announced that the United States had entered the war.

turned turtle: turned upside down

superstructure: the part of a ship that is above the main deck

hull: the main body of a ship

John Garcia joined the service a year after the bombing of Pearl Harbor at the age of 17. He went on to fight in the Philippines and Japan. After World War II ended, he joined the police force in Washington, D.C., where he worked for 15 years. Garcia was living in Los Angeles in 1984 when he was interviewed about his experiences at Pearl Harbor.

From *"The Good War": An Oral History of World War Two*, pp. 19–24, by Studs Terkel. Copyright © 1984 by Studs Terkel. Reprinted by permission of Pantheon Books, a division of Random House, Inc.

Dec. 7, 1941 10:00 A.M.

8:17 A.M. (3:17 A.M. in Washington) President Roosevelt is notified of the attack.

8:40 A.M. The second wave of Japanese aircraft joins the attack.

10:00 A.M. The attack ends.

Forced to Leave Our Home

Margaret Takahashi

Under army escort Japanese Americans were led to trains bound for relocation camps. Friends and relatives watched from above.

The Japanese bombing of Pearl Harbor in 1941 made many Americans angry. Some thought that Japanese people in the United States could not be trusted. In 1942 the United States forced nearly 110,000 Japanese people into **internment camps**. Most of them had homes on the West Coast. About two thirds were American citizens. Margaret Takahashi and her family were among these people.

internment camps: temporary places set up to house Japanese Americans. Residents of the camps were treated like prisoners of war.

nursery: store for growing and selling plants

Covina, California: a town on the West Coast

When the war started I was married and had two children and was expecting a third. My husband, Jimmy, was gardening and going to school studying landscape architecture, and we had started a **nursery** in Los Angeles. We had been working on it day and night for about a year, and we were just starting to sell. Then everything went up in the air.

I was born in Japan. My mother was from Ireland and my father was from Japan. They met when my father came to the United States to go to college and my mother came from Ireland to work. They met on a train, fell in love and got married. They had three children; then they went on a visit to Japan and had me. They thought if they stayed and I was a boy I'd inherit, but since I was a girl, forget it. Plus we were mixed, and they don't like mixed people in Japan. So they came back to the United States.

Jimmy's parents were both Japanese, but he was an American citizen, for he was born in **Covina, California**. Anyone born here was a citizen. Since I was born in

1941		
July 1941 The United States cuts off exports to Japan.	**Nov. 1941** Japanese leaders negotiate with the United States as Japan secretly prepares to attack.	**Dec. 1941** The Japanese attack Pearl Harbor. The United States enters World War II.

Japan, I wasn't, and Japanese were not allowed to become **naturalized** at that time. But we didn't feel Japanese. We felt American. That was the way we were raised.

After Pearl Harbor we started to get worried because the newspapers were **agitating** and printing all those stories all the time. And people were getting angrier. You kept hearing awful rumors. You heard that people were getting their houses burned down and we were afraid that those things might happen to us. . . . Your whole future seemed in question. The longer the war dragged on, the worse the feeling got.

When the **evacuation** order finally came I was relieved. Lots of people were relieved, because you were taken care of. You wouldn't have all this worry. . . .

We had the baby on Easter Sunday, and it was a boy, and I was really happy about having a son. I had two daughters first, and I had always wanted a boy. Then three weeks later we were evacuated.

You could only take one suitcase apiece, but people who had gone to camp before us were able to tell us what to bring, so we were a little better off than others. My husband bought foot lockers, so our luggage was pretty big and we took sheets and things that the other people hadn't taken.

We sold our nursery stock to a different nursery, and all the **lath houses** we'd built, but we didn't get much for them. The rest of the stuff we stored with a friend who was reliable. A lot of people I knew gave things to friends to keep and they never saw the friends again, but ours was a good one.

The day we were taken to camp we had to go to a special **designated** place to get the bus. This friend of ours took me and the baby so that we wouldn't have to walk. Most people just walked. We got on the bus and everybody was sitting there, and I was thinking, Gee, everybody's so brave, nobody's crying, and I wasn't going to cry either, because Japanese frown on weakness, so I wouldn't look at anybody. And then this colored lady came up

Newspaper headlines like the one above made people fear Japanese Americans. Some thought all Japanese were spies.

1945

May 1942 Japanese Americans are sent to internment camps.

Sept. 1945 Japan surrenders. World War II ends.

and looked in the bus window and she said, "Oh, look at the poor thing, she has a tiny baby." And then I started to bawl, and I bawled the whole way to camp. I felt like a fool, because nobody else cried. They didn't even cry when I cried. They just sat zombielike. They could hold it in that much.

We were taken to Santa Anita Racetrack, and they had built **barracks** for us. The first people who were taken to Santa Anita had to live in the stables. They had it bad, because the stables had a lot of fleas, and they smelled. But they had showers. We had to walk there to take showers and wash at first, and it was almost a mile from our barracks.

When we first arrived, we were examined by doctors, and they made you open your mouth and I didn't want to open my mouth, so this doctor pulled it open, and I kicked him in the leg. I felt good about that.

The first meal was spaghetti without meat, and yams. Plain boiled yams. I'll always remember that. Nothing tasted good. The whole time we were in camp, nothing tasted good.

We were in Santa Anita a few months, and my five-year-old, Winkie, my oldest daughter, came up to me one day and said, "Momma, I don't like this neighborhood. Can't we move?" And I just felt we had to get out of there. We had heard a rumor that **Father Flanagan of Boys Town** was hiring people. . . . So my husband wrote him a letter, and he wrote back right away and told us to come. That was Father Flanagan's mission in life—to take the rejected or unwanted. He had a home for homeless boys near Omaha and he needed workers, for all of his workers were being called up to the Army.

We wrote back and forth for several months, and nothing happened. We just couldn't get permission to leave. . . . So finally we telegraphed to the head of the camp. They were going to move the whole camp out in a few days. Our group was to go to **Amache, Colorado**, and we said, "Oh, God, we aren't going to get to go to Boys Town." It was very tense.

A child sits atop her parents' belongings as she waits to be moved to a relocation camp.

To pass the time at relocation camps many Japanese Americans planted gardens and worked on their small cottages to make them more livable.

I thought they wouldn't let us go. But finally they sent a telegram and we got permission. . . .

We arrived in Boys Town at night, and Father Flanagan met us at the train. . . . He was a very tall, gentle, warm man. When you first met him, you could feel this warmth. I've never felt that from another human being. He was so full of love that it radiated out of him. It was startling.

Then my husband came three days later, and we settled in this farmhouse on Boys Town property and started right in to work. We lived on a real farm with a pump and **cistern**, and there was a place you could plant your garden. We had a **victory garden**. . . . We learned to can, and to cook on a cook stove, and what a real winter was. I just loved it there. I didn't want to come back, but my husband wanted to be his own boss, so after the war, in 1947, we moved back to Los Angeles.

When I think back to the **internment**, I want to call it a concentration camp, but it wasn't. We have a neighbor who escaped from **Auschwitz** during the war, and there's no comparison. In our life it was only four months, and that's not long.

But the evacuation did change our philosophy. It made you feel that you knew what it was to die, to go somewhere you couldn't take anything but what you had inside you. And so it strengthened you. I think from then on we were very strong. I don't think anything could get us down now.

cistern: underground tank for storing rainwater

victory garden: vegetable garden planted by Americans to help ease food shortages during the war

internment: the time spent in the camp; confinement

Auschwitz: a prisoner camp in Germany; concentration camp

Many Japanese were given only 48 hours notice to leave home. They had to sell their houses and businesses quickly. Government officials shipped them to internment camps. These camps were made up of barracks with barbed wire around them. The Japanese lived there like prisoners for about a year. In 1989 the U.S. government decided to give $20,000 to each Japanese American who had been held in an internment camp.

Reprinted by permission of The Putnam Publishing Group from *The Homefront: America During WWII*, pp. 104–9. Copyright © 1984 by Mark Harris, Franklin Mitchell, and Steven J. Schechter.

A New President Writes Home

> " . . . hostilities will cease on all fronts at midnight tonight. "
>
> **Harry S. Truman**

Harry Truman greets his 92-year-old mother, Martha Truman. It was her first visit since he became president in 1945.

On April 12, 1945, in the midst of World War II, President Franklin D. Roosevelt died suddenly. Vice President Harry S. Truman became the new president. Several weeks later the German armed forces collapsed. Adolf Hitler killed himself soon after. Germany surrendered on May 7. The next morning Truman wrote this letter to his mother and sister. ∾

May 8, 1945: V-E Day (Victory in Europe Day), the end of the war in Europe

Mama & Mary: Truman's mother, Martha Ellen Young Truman, and his sister, Mary Jane Truman

hostilities: unfriendly acts

May 8, 1945

Dear **Mama & Mary:**

I am sixty-one this morning, and I slept in the President's room in the White House last night. They have finished the painting and have some of the furniture in place. I'm hoping it will all be ready for you by Friday. My expensive gold pen doesn't work as well as it should.

This will be a historical day. At 9:00 o'clock this morning I must make a broadcast to the country: announcing the German surrender. The papers were signed yesterday morning and **hostilities** will cease on all fronts at midnight tonight. Isn't that some birthday present?

Jan. 1945

Jan. 1945	Apr. 1945	May 1945
F. D. Roosevelt begins fourth presidential term. Harry S. Truman becomes vice president.	President Roosevelt dies. Truman becomes president.	Germany surrenders. The war in Europe is over. Truman declares May 8 as Victory in Europe Day.

Have had one heck of a time with the **Prime Minister of Great Britain**. He, **Stalin** and the **U.S. President** made an agreement to release the news all at once from the three capitals at an hour that would fit us all. We agreed on 9 A.M. Washington time which is 3 P.M. London and 4 P.M. Moscow time.

Mr. Churchill began calling me at daylight to know if we shouldn't make an immediate release without considering the Russians. He was refused and then he kept pushing me to talk to Stalin. He finally had to stick to the agreed plan—but he was mad as a wet hen.

Things have moved at a terrific rate here since April 12. Never a day has gone by that some **momentous** decision didn't have to be made. So far luck has been with me. I hope it keeps up. It can't stay with me forever however and I hope when the mistake comes it won't be too great to remedy. We are looking forward to a grand visit with you. I may not be able to come for you as planned but I'm sending the safest, finest plane and all kinds of help so please don't disappoint me.

Lots & lots of love to you both.

Harry

Prime Minister of Great Britain: chief official of the British government; here, Winston Churchill

Stalin: Joseph Stalin, Communist dictator of the Soviet Union

U.S. President: Franklin Delano Roosevelt, who was president before Truman

momentous: very important

Truman had been vice president only 82 days when he became president of the United States. He faced important decisions that would affect the end of the war. After Germany surrendered, Truman met with Churchill and Stalin at Potsdam, Germany. Here they discussed the fate of Germany. They also talked about how to end the war with Japan. On his way home from Potsdam, Truman made one of the most difficult decisions ever faced by one person. He ordered American fliers to drop an atomic bomb on the Japanese city of Hiroshima. Another bomb was dropped three days later on Nagasaki. Eight days later, on August 14, Japan agreed to end the war. On September 2, Japan signed a formal surrender.

From *Letters in American History*, ed. H. Jack Lang (New York: Harmony Books, 1982), p. 96.

	Sept. 1945
Aug. 1945 American fliers drop atomic bombs on Hiroshima and Nagasaki.	**Sept. 1945** World War II is over.

BREAKING NEW GROUND

Space travel has opened the door to a new frontier. This view of Earth is quite different from what the early explorers saw on their voyages of discovery.

segregated: separated by race

integrating: bringing blacks and whites together in order to end segregation

civil rights: the rights of all citizens to enjoy life, liberty, property, and protection of the law

When World War II was over, people were eager to rebuild their lives. In the 1950s millions of couples married and had children. Growing families meant a growing need for housing, clothing, and other consumer goods. Businesses grew larger to meet this need. Jobs were plentiful, and most people lived well.

But in the 1950s most black Americans were not living well. Nor were they treated equally throughout the country. Many white people wanted to maintain a way of life that kept blacks and whites **segregated**. In many places, blacks had to use separate schools, drinking fountains, and restaurants. In 1954 the Supreme Court ruled that segregation in public schools was unconstitutional. The Court said that school districts had to start **integrating** their schools. This gave strength to the **civil rights** movement. Black and white Americans joined together to fight for equal rights for all.

1950	1960	1970

1957 Federal court orders Central High School in Little Rock, Arkansas, to begin integration.

Americans also began another struggle. They began to seek **superiority** in space. The Soviet Union had launched the first **artificial satellite**, *Sputnik I*, in 1957. Many Americans thought the United States should have been first in space. So in 1961 President John F. Kennedy set an important goal. He said the United States would send the first person to the moon by 1970. This goal was met on July 20, 1969, when Neil Armstrong stepped onto the moon. Now Americans have set even higher goals in space exploration.

The first men to walk on the moon were Neil Armstrong and Buzz Aldrin. This photo shows Aldrin on the moon. Armstrong is reflected in his visor.

The goals of equality at home and exploration in space are still important issues as the United States looks toward the twenty-first century. In this unit three individuals describe the story of our progress at home and among the stars.

- **Elizabeth Eckford** describes what it was like to be the first black student to try to enter Central High School in Little Rock, Arkansas.
- **Sally Ride** describes what it was like to go to space aboard the space shuttle *Challenger*.
- President **Jimmy Carter's** words of peace and hope travel with the *Voyager* probes in space.

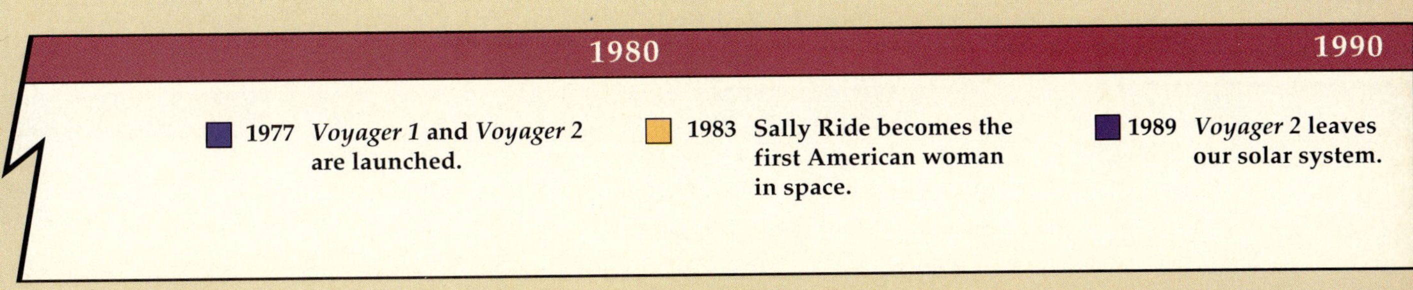

Crisis at Little Rock

❝ The crowd moved in closer and then began to follow me, calling me names. I still wasn't afraid. ❞

Elizabeth Eckford

Elizabeth Eckford was stopped by National Guardsmen as she tried to enter an all-white school in Little Rock, Arkansas, in 1957.

In 1954 the United States Supreme Court decided that black and white children should attend the same schools. But many white people did not agree. They tried to keep nine black students out of all-white Central High School in Little Rock, Arkansas. Elizabeth Eckford was the first black student to arrive at school. She tells what happened on September 4, 1957. ∞

Superintendent Blossom: Virgil T. Blossom, head of the Little Rock School District

mob: a large crowd, especially an excited crowd that pays no attention to law and order

"You remember the day before we were to go in, we met **Superintendent Blossom** at the school board office. He told us what the **mob** might say and do but he never told us we wouldn't have any protection. He told our parents not to come because he wouldn't be able to protect the children if they did.

"That night I was so excited I couldn't sleep. The next morning I was about the first one up. While I was pressing my black and white dress—I had made it to wear on the first day of school—my little brother turned on the TV set. They started telling about a large crowd gathered at the school. The man on TV said he wondered if we were going to show up that morning. Mother called from the kitchen, where she was fixing breakfast, 'Turn that TV off!' She was so upset and worried. I wanted to comfort her, so I said, 'Mother, don't worry.'

"Dad was walking back and forth, from room to room, with a sad expression. He was chewing on his pipe and he had a cigar in his hand, but he didn't light either one. It would have been funny, only he was so nervous.

"Before I left home Mother called us into the living-room. She said we should have a word of prayer. Then I caught the bus and got off a block from the school. I saw a large crowd of people standing across the street from the soldiers guarding **Central**. As I walked on, the crowd suddenly got very quiet. Superintendent Blossom had told us to enter by the front door. I looked at all the people and thought, 'Maybe I will be safer if I walk down the block to the front entrance behind the guards.'

"At the corner I tried to pass through the long line of guards around the school so as to enter the grounds behind them. One of the guards pointed across the street. So I pointed in the same direction and asked whether he meant for me to cross the street and walk down. He nodded 'yes.' So, I walked across the street **conscious** of the crowd that stood there, but they moved away from me.

"For a moment all I could hear was the shuffling of their feet. Then someone shouted, 'Here she comes, get ready!' I moved away from the crowd on the sidewalk and into the street. If the mob came at me I could then cross back over so the guards could protect me.

"The crowd moved in closer and then began to follow me, calling me names. I still wasn't afraid. Just a little bit nervous. Then my knees started to shake all of a sudden and I wondered

Angry townspeople and students gathered in front of Central High School to stop black students from entering.

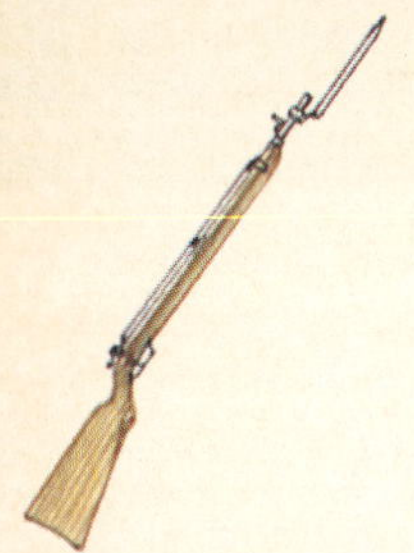

whether I could make it to the center entrance a block away. It was the longest block I ever walked in my whole life.

"Even so, I still wasn't too scared because all the time I kept thinking that the guards would protect me.

"When I got right in front of the school, I went up to a guard again. But this time he just looked straight ahead and didn't move to let me pass him. I didn't know what to do. Then I looked and saw that the path leading to the front entrance was a little further ahead. So I walked until I was right in front of the path to the front door.

"I stood looking at the school —it looked so big! Just then the guards let some white students go through.

"The crowd was quiet. I guess they were waiting to see what was going to happen. When I was able to steady my knees, I walked up to the guard who had let the white students in. He too didn't move. When I tried to squeeze past him, he raised his **bayonet** and then the other guards closed in and they raised their bayonets.

"They **glared** at me with a mean look and I was very frightened and didn't know what to do. I turned around and the crowd came toward me.

"They moved closer and closer. Somebody started yelling, '**Lynch** her! Lynch her!'

"I tried to see a friendly face somewhere in the mob—someone who maybe would help. I looked into the face of an old woman and it seemed a kind face, but when I looked at her again, she spat on me.

"They came closer, shouting, 'No [black girl] is going to get in our school. Get out of here!'

"I turned back to the guards but their faces told me I wouldn't get help from them. Then I looked down the block and saw a bench at the bus stop. I thought, 'If I can only get there I will be safe.' I don't know why the bench seemed a safe place to me, but I started walking toward it. I tried to close my mind to what they were shouting, and kept saying to myself, 'If I can only make it to the bench I will be safe.'

"When I finally got there, I

On September 24, nine black students once again tried to enter Central High School. This time they were escorted into the school by federal troops.

don't think I could have gone another step. I sat down and the mob crowded up and began shouting all over again. Someone hollered, 'Drag her over to this tree! Let's take care of [her].' Just then a white man sat down beside me, put his arm around me and patted my shoulder. He raised my chin and said, 'Don't let them see you cry.'

"Then, a white lady—she was very nice—she came over to me on the bench. She spoke to me but I don't remember now what she said. She put me on the bus and sat next to me. She asked me my name and tried to talk to me but I don't think I answered. I can't remember much about the bus ride, but the next thing I remember I was standing in front of the School for the Blind, where Mother works.

"I thought, 'Maybe she isn't here. But she has to be here!' So I ran upstairs, and I think some teachers tried to talk to me, but I kept running until I reached Mother's classroom.

"Mother was standing at the window with her head bowed, but she must have sensed I was there because she turned around. She looked as if she had been crying, and I wanted to tell her I was all right. But I couldn't speak. She put her arms around me and I cried."

A mother and child sit on the steps of the Supreme Court. The newspaper announces the court's landmark decision to allow black students to go to white schools.

Elizabeth and the other black students stayed home from school for three weeks. Then, on September 24, President Eisenhower sent soldiers to take them to Central High. He ordered the Arkansas National Guard to protect them. But even that was not enough. The students put up with insults, beatings, and even bomb attacks on their homes. But they stayed at Central. The first victory had been won, and the fight for equality continued.

From *The Long Shadow of Little Rock* by Daisy Bates. Copyright © 1962 by Daisy Bates. Reprinted by permission of David McKay Co., a division of Random House, Inc.

To Space and Back

> " 3 . . . 2 . . . 1 . . . The rockets light! The shuttle leaps off the launch pad. . . . "
>
> **Sally Ride**

Sally Ride was one of six women chosen for the astronaut class of 1978. She went through training at the Johnson Space Center.

In June 1983 Sally Ride became the first woman from the United States to travel in space. Ride and four other astronauts made a six-day flight aboard the space shuttle *Challenger*. During the mission the astronauts launched communications satellites, did experiments, and tested the shuttle's robot arm. Sally Ride describes what it was like to go to space and back.

Launch minus one hour. We check to make sure that we are strapped in properly, that oxygen will flow into our helmets, that our radio communication with **Mission Control** is working, and that our pencils and our books— the procedure manuals and checklists we'll need during liftoff— are attached to something to keep them from shaking loose. Then we wait.

The technicians close the hatch and then head for safety three miles away. We're all alone on the launch pad.

Launch minus seven minutes. The walkway with the white room at the end slowly pulls away. Far below us the power units start whirring, sending a shudder through the shuttle. We close the **visors** on our helmets and begin to breathe from the oxygen supply. Then the space shuttle quivers again as its launch engines slowly move into position for blast-off.

Launch minus 10 seconds . . . 9 . . . 8 . . . 7 . . . The three launch engines light. The shuttle shakes and strains at the bolts holding it to the launch pad. The computers

1958		
1958 The United States launches its first satellite, *Explorer I*.	**1962** U.S. astronaut John Glenn becomes the first American to orbit Earth.	**1969** U.S. astronauts Neil Armstrong and Edwin Aldrin walk on the moon.

check the engines. It isn't up to us anymore—the computers will decide whether we launch.

3 . . . 2 . . . 1 . . . The rockets light! The shuttle leaps off the launch pad in a cloud of steam and a trail of fire. Inside, the ride is rough and loud. Our heads are rattling around inside our helmets. We can barely hear the voices from Mission Control in our headsets above the thunder of the rockets and engines. For an instant I wonder if everything is working right. But there's no more time to wonder, and no time to be scared.

In only a few seconds we zoom past the clouds. Two minutes later the rockets burn out, and with a brilliant whitish-orange flash, they fall away from the shuttle as it streaks on toward space. Suddenly the ride becomes very, very smooth and quiet. The shuttle is still attached to the big tank, and the launch engines are pushing us out of the Earth's **atmosphere**. The sky is black. All we can see of the trail of fire behind us is a faint, **pulsating** glow through the top window.

Launch plus six minutes. The force pushing us against the backs of our seats steadily increases. We can barely move because we're being held in place by a force of 3 g's—three times the force of gravity we feel on Earth. At first we don't mind it—we've all felt much more than that when we've done **acrobatics** in our jet training airplanes. But that lasted only a few seconds, and this seems to go on forever. After a couple of minutes of 3 g's, we're uncomfortable, straining to hold our books on our laps and craning our necks against the force to read the instruments. I find myself wishing we'd hurry up and get into orbit.

Launch plus eight and one-half minutes. The launch engines cut off. Suddenly the force is gone, and we **lurch** forward in our seats. During the next few minutes the empty fuel tank drops away and falls to Earth, and we are very busy getting the shuttle ready to enter orbit. But we're not too busy to notice that our books and pencils are floating in midair. We're in space! . . .

The best part of being in space is being weightless. It feels

Powerful rockets lifted the shuttle *Challenger* and its crew into space at the Kennedy Space Center in Florida.

atmosphere: the air that surrounds Earth

pulsating: alternating from bright to dim

acrobatics: hard tricks; stunts

lurch: lean suddenly

1981 The United States launches the first reusable crewed spacecraft, the space shuttle *Columbia.*

1983 Sally Ride becomes the first U.S. woman in space.

Sally Ride floats weightlessly on the flight deck of the *Challenger.* Three calculators drift near her in midair.

wonderful to be able to float without effort; to **slither** up, down, and around the inside of the shuttle just like a seal; to be upside down as often as I'm right side up and have it make no difference. . . .

When I'm weightless, some things don't change. My heart beats at about the same rate as it does on Earth. I can still swallow and digest food. My eyes, ears, nose, and taste buds work fine; I see, hear, smell, and taste things just as I do at home.

I *look* a little different, though—all astronauts do. Since the **fluid** in our bodies is not pulled toward our feet as it is on Earth, more of this fluid stays in our faces and upper bodies. This makes our faces a little fatter and gives us puffy-looking cheeks. We are also about an inch taller while in orbit because in weightlessness our spines are not compressed. . . .

During my first day in space, I had to learn how to move around. I started out trying to "swim" through the air, but that didn't work at all; air isn't **dense**, the way water is, and I felt silly dog-paddling in the air, going nowhere. Before long I discovered that I had to push off from one of the walls if I wanted to get across the room. At first I would push off a little too hard and crash into the opposite wall, but I soon learned to wind my way around with very gentle pushes. . . .

Inside the space shuttle, astronauts perform experiments exploring ways to make new substances —medicines, metals, or crystals— in weightlessness. We also record **data** about our own bodies to help scientists understand the effects of weightlessness. . . .

The day before the shuttle returns to Earth, astronauts have to put away all loose equipment. Cameras, food trays, and books will stay attached to the ceiling or walls with **Velcro** as long as they are weightless, but they would come crashing to the floor if we left them out during **re-entry**. . . . An amazing number of lost pencils and books turn up floating behind wall and ceiling panels. . . .

Four or five hours before landing, we begin to drink liquid— four or more big glasses each—and take salt pills to keep the liquid in our bodies. We have to do this because our bodies have gotten rid of some water during the flight to adjust to weightlessness. . . .

We also put on "g-suits," pants that can be **inflated** to keep the blood from pooling in our legs. If we begin to feel lightheaded as we re-enter the atmosphere, a sign that not enough blood is reaching the brain, we can inflate our g-suits.

Finally we strap ourselves into our seats, connect our helmets to the oxygen supply, and fire the shuttle's small space engines. This "de-orbit burn" slows the shuttle down and brings us back into Earth's atmosphere. . . .

Gravity slowly begins pulling us into our seats, and we start to feel heavier and heavier. Since we are used to weightless books, pencils, arms, and heads, all these things now seem very heavy to us. It's an effort even to lift a hand. . . .

The pilot lowers the landing gear when the spaceplane is only a few hundred feet above the ground. The landing gear slows us down, but we still land at about two hundred miles per hour— quite a bit faster than most airplanes. The rear wheels touch the runway first, so gently that inside we can't even be sure we've landed. Then the nose wheel comes down with a hard thump, and we know we're back on Earth.

Space shuttles are launched like rockets but can land on a runway like a jet. Sally Ride and the *Challenger* crew landed at Edwards Air Force Base in California when they returned from space.

In October 1984 Sally Ride made her second trip into space, once again aboard the space shuttle *Challenger*. On this mission the astronauts used the robot arm to launch a satellite that measures how the sun affects our weather. Ride left the astronaut program in 1987 to become a researcher at the Stanford University Center for International Security and Arms Control in California.

Message Into the Cosmos

Gold-plated records were mounted on *Voyagers 1* and *2* before they were launched into space. The "Sounds of Earth" recordings contained messages and pictures.

The United States launched *Voyagers 1* and 2, identical unmanned space probes, in 1977. The probes flew by several planets in our solar system to collect information. Then they sailed on into space. No one knows how long or how far they will travel. Each probe carries an electronic recording of sounds and pictures of Earth. The recording also contains this message from former President Jimmy Carter.

This Voyager spacecraft was constructed by the United States of America. We are a community of 240 million human beings among the more than 4 billion who inhabit the planet Earth. We human beings are still divided into nation states, but these states are rapidly becoming a single global civilization.

We cast this message into the **cosmos.** It is likely to survive a billion years into our future, when our civilization is profoundly altered and the surface of the Earth may be vastly changed.

Of the 200 billion stars in the Milky Way galaxy, some—perhaps many—may have inhabited planets and **spacefaring** civilizations. If one such civilization **intercepts** Voyager and can understand these recorded contents, here is our message:

This is a present from a small distant world, a token of our sounds, our science, our images, our music, our thoughts and our

cosmos:
the universe

spacefaring:
having to do with
space travel

intercepts: stops
or catches along
the way

1977		
1977 United States launches space probes (*Voyager 2*, Aug. 20; *Voyager 1*, Sept. 5).	**1979** The probes fly by Jupiter (*Voyager 1*, March; *Voyager 2*, July).	**Nov. 1980** *Voyager 1* flies by Saturn and then heads out of the solar system.

feelings. We are attempting to survive our time so we may live into yours.

We hope someday, having solved the problems we face, to join a community of **galactic** civilizations. This record represents our hope and our determination, and our good will in a vast and awesome universe.

Jimmy Carter
President
United States of America

The *Voyager* (top left) gathered information on Saturn as it passed by on its journey through space. The computer-generated picture (top right) shows six of Saturn's 21 moons. Color was added to a photo of Saturn (bottom left) to show the different gases present on Saturn's surface. Saturn's rings (bottom right) are made of ice particles—some as small as a speck of dust, others as large as a house.

Voyagers 1 and *2* are flying out of our solar system to an unknown destination. Perhaps they will travel for billions of years. Perhaps they will be destroyed by a collision with a star or asteroid. What if they really *are* intercepted by another civilization? Will someone understand our message of hope? Will someone listen to the sounds of our Earth?

From *Letters in American History*, ed. H. Jack Lang (New York: Harmony Books, 1982), p. 122.

		1989
Aug. 1981 *Voyager* 2 flies by Saturn.	**Jan. 1986** *Voyager* 2 flies by Uranus.	**Aug. 1989** *Voyager* 2 flies by Neptune and then heads out of the solar system.

INDEX

PHOTO CREDITS

Table of Contents: **iii** (top to bottom) Unit 1: Nasjonalgalleriet, Oslo. Unit 2: The Bettmann Archive. Unit 3: Massachusetts Historical Society. Unit 4: Special Collections Division, University of Washington Libraries. Unit 5: The Bettmann Archive. **iv** (top to bottom) Unit 6: The Granger Collection, New York. Unit 7: Brown Brothers. Unit 8: The Granger Collection, New York. Unit 9: National Archives. Unit 10: NASA.

Introduction: Theodore Roosevelt Collection, Harvard College Library.

Unit One: 2: The Bettmann Archive. 3: The Granger Collection, New York. 4, 5: Nasjonalgalleriet, Oslo. 7, 8, 9, 10, 11: The Granger Collection, New York. 13: The Bettmann Archive. 14, 15: The Granger Collection, New York.

Unit Two: 17, 18: The Bettmann Archive. 20, 21: The Granger Collection, New York. 22: American Antiquarian Society. 24, 26, 27: The Granger Collection, New York.

Unit Three: 29: The Granger Collection, New York. 30: (top) The Bettmann Archive; (bottom) The Granger Collection, New York. 33: The Bettmann Archive. 34: (both) Massachusetts Historical Society. 35, 36: The Granger Collection, New York. 37: The Bettmann Archive. 38, 39: The Granger Collection, New York.

Unit Four: 41: The Granger Collection, New York. 42: Special Collections Division, University of Washington Libraries. 43, 44: American Museum of Natural History. 45: Special Collections Division, University of Washington Libraries. 46: National Park Service, Scott's Bluff National Monument. 47: The Granger Collection, New York. 49: The Bettmann Archive. 50, 51: The Granger Collection, New York.

Unit Five: 53: The Bettmann Archive. 54: National Portrait Gallery, Smithsonian Institution. 55: The Granger Collection, New York. 56: The Bettmann Archive. 57: The Granger Collection, New York. 58: The Bettmann Archive. 60: The Granger Collection, New York. 63: National Archives.

Unit Six: 65, 66, 68, 69, 70, 71, 72: The Granger Collection, New York. 73: Thomas Gilcrease Institute, Tulsa, Okla. 74, 75: The Granger Collection, New York.

Unit Seven: 77, 78: The Granger Collection, New York. 79: Museum of the City of New York. 80: The Bettmann Archive. 81: Brown Brothers. 82, 83: Sears, Roebuck, and Co. catalog (as published by Chelsea House Publishers). 84: Theodore Roosevelt Collection, Harvard College Library. 85: Library of Congress.

Unit Eight: 89: The Granger Collection, New York. 90, 91, 92: The Bettmann Archive. 93, 94: The Granger Collection, New York. 95: Tennessee State Library and Archives. 96: UPI/Bettmann Newsphotos. 97:(all photos) Library of Congress. 98: The Bettmann Archive.

Unit Nine: 101: The Granger Collection, New York. 102: National Archives. 103, 104, 105: UPI/Bettmann Newsphotos. 106, 107: National Archives. 108: UPI/Bettmann Newsphotos.

Unit Ten: 110, 111: NASA. 112, 113: UPI/Bettmann Newsphotos. 114: AP/Wide World Photos. 115: UPI/Bettmann Newsphotos. 116, 117, 118, 119: NASA. 120: Kennedy Space Center. 121: (all photos) Jet Propulsion Laboratory, California Institute of Technology.